**FAMILY GUY**

# Peter Griffin's
# Guide
## to the
# Holidays

### By Peter Griffin

## Helped into Print by Danny Smith

## Based on the Series Created
## by Seth MacFarlane

HARPER

NEW YORK • LONDON • TORONTO • SYDNEY

**PETER'S DEDICATION** To my wife, Lois, who I still can't believe I'm having sex with, and who I think Bruce Springsteen was thinking about when he sang, "Jesus, send some good women to save all your clowns." And, Lois, I really hope this dedication brings you joy and happiness for the holidays. Because I just now realized that I forgot to buy you a present again, and by now I'm pretty sure all the stores are closed. So this is it. —P. G.

**DANNY'S DEDICATION** To Big Hal, who taught me how to love and laugh. To the Headman, who taught me how to write. And to Lisa Smith, who taught me just about everything else. But most of all, to Gramma Nan, the architect, builder, and provider of every glorious Christmas I have ever known. In spite of what we've been told, Santa Claus did not live at the North Pole. She lived at my house in Greenville, Rhode Island. —D. S.

FAMILY GUY: PETER GRIFFIN'S GUIDE TO THE HOLIDAYS. Copyright © 2007 by Twentieth Century Fox Film Corporation. All rights reserved. Printed in the United States of America. No part of this book may be used or reproduced in any manner whatsoever without written permission except in the case of brief quotations embodied in critical articles and reviews. For information address HarperCollins Publishers, 10 East 53rd Street, New York, NY 10022.

Use of KISS likenesses, makeup, and costumes on page 82-83 courtesy of KISS Catalog, Ltd. All rights reserved.

HarperCollins books may be purchased for educational, business, or sales promotional use. For information please write: Special Markets Department, HarperCollins Publishers, 10 East 53rd Street, New York, NY 10022.

FIRST EDITION

Designed by Timothy Shaner, nightanddaydesign.biz

Printed on acid-free paper

Library of Congress Cataloging-in-Publication Data is available upon request.

ISBN: 978-0-06-137315-2    ISBN-10: 0-06-137315-X

07 08 09 10 11 ❖ 10 9 8 7 6 5 4 3 2 1

# DISCLAIMER

Okay, before we get started I've been asked to point out that the views represented in this book are not the views of HarperCollins Publishers. Nor are they the views of the Fox Broadcasting Company. And you should be damned happy for that, because trust me, for the most part they are a group of truly humorless people. I know this because I had to sit in a room with a whole bunch of them when we were working out a deal to do this book and it was just awful. It was a lot like being in church, except nobody laughed when I farted. Well, except for me, and that gets me back to the original point, which is that they didn't write this book, I did. So don't go calling them or bothering them if something I say in this thing puts a hair across your ass. Just lighten up, stupid. It's all for fun. And even if it weren't, what are you gonna do—punch me? That'd be one hell of a punch considering I'm a fictional cartoon character. And you can rim my hairy bum for all I care, which is my view at this time, but is *not* the view of HarperCollins Publishers or the Fox Broadcasting Company, who by now I'm certain are already regretting their decision to let me do this.

Holy crap, writing is even harder than reading.

 **HAPPY HOLIDAYS FROM OUR FAMILY TO YOURS!**

# Contents

# Season's Greetings from Quahog, Rhode Island

**Hi, neighbor!** This is your old pal Peter Griffin. Thank you for welcoming me into your home. I'm sure that I am in your home because if you're reading this, then you just bought this book and have taken it home to read. You *have* bought this book, right? 'Cause I'd hate to think I'm talking to one of those douche bags who stands around in the store, grabbing books and reading up a storm and bending all the pages and then putting 'em back like this is the freakin' library or something. Is that what you're doing? Because that's a little like piracy, which may look good on Johnny Depp, but only makes you look like someone who is helping to screw up the American economy, as well as aiding and abetting the terrorists. And if *that* is the case, then I'm not saying another word until you trot your showy, oh-look-at-me-I'm-so-smart-I-can-read-right-here-in-the-store ass up to the counter and pay for this piece of crap. Then, take it home, find a comfy chair, and start over. But skip the part where I call you a douche bag, because by then your actions will have made it a moot point.

> Remember, Santa is watching you! And so is the government! So watch your step, you little bastards!

Well, it's that time of year again! Can you feel it? The big tree in the center of town is being decorated at the expense of the taxpayers, regardless of their ideologies or religious beliefs. Herbert, the kind old man down the street, is once again filling the pockets of his tattered old bathrobe with gumdrops and hard candies, and generously allowing the neighborhood kids to go pawing at him and fishing around in there to their heart's content. Ahh . . . I can already see the warm twinkle in his eye, and the joyful smile on his gross old wrinkly mouth, all hanging open with food in the corners of it and smelling like PoliGrip. And as a giddy cackle wheezes out of that ugly old bastard, a soft blast of white steam rises from his gaping, gap-toothed piehole, reminding us that once again, all over Quahog, there's a nip in the air. And when I say "nip in the air," I'm not remembering Pearl Harbor, or any time Tara Reid walked down a red carpet with one of her drunk boobs hanging out for all of us to see and enjoy. No, I'm talking about that magic time in Quahog when Jack Frost is nipping at your nuts, when the treetops glisten, and we're all pissin', to write our name in yellow snow. That's right! It's the holiday season! Christmastime—the greatest, most wicked-awesome, dipsolucious season there is. Now, don't get me wrong, I love all the holidays—Easter Sunday, Super Bowl Sunday, and even Columbus Day, which was invented by the greeting card companies so that Italian guys could feel even more proud of themselves and go "Ohh!" like Tony Soprano when they point at you and smugly take credit for discovering America, when in fact what they're really known for, mostly, is rooting for the Yankees, talking with their hands, and shooting each other in the back of the head. But of all God's holidays great and small, pound for pound, there is nothing that compares with the joy and happiness of Christmas. Nothing. Nada, pal. Zippo, zilch—and whatever other words you can come up with that mean "nothing," because I'm already out.

And I know what you're saying right now, because we've known each other for at least two or three pages. You're saying, "Nothing? Nothing is better than Christmas? Now, hold on there, Peter. Just a second. What about sex with Jessica Alba? Huh? What about that?" Well, don't think I haven't thought about that, Einstein, because I have. I have thought about sex with Jessica Alba. I think about it practically every day, and have been ever since the first time I saw her in *Dark Angel*. In fact, at this moment, right now, I almost can't think about anything else, so thanks for bringing it up, jackass. Oh my God, is she not awesome? How freakin' hot is she? And how stupid are those idiots who made that movie *Fantastic Four*? They're all, like, "Hey . . . here's an idea. Let's have Jessica Alba in our movie . . . but we'll make her *invisible*!" "Yeah! Let's take this ridiculously smokin' hot chick that everybody wants to look at and have

I'm not sure who "The Little Drummer Boy" was—but it sure as hell wasn't Tommy Lee, because I saw that video of him with Pamela Anderson, and believe me, that guy is not little. He's huge! Freakishly huge.

her play the Fantastic Invisible Girl." Great. Good casting, guys. Look, don't get me wrong, I don't claim to be some kind of Spielberg or Cecil-and-Beanie DeMille, but even I know that all the invisible roles in Hollywood should be saved for Camryn Manheim, or whatever's left of Cher. But I digest. Yes, we all can agree that few things could be better than sex with Jessica Alba. But hold your horses, John Q. Public— for I will now tell you why Christmas is even better. And in doing so, I will use the debating skills I honed as a teenager during the three weeks I was on the James Woods High School Debate Squad, before I got thrown off and banned for life for punching out a girl from the Woonsocket High team at the close of what I still say was my best debate ever.

Point A: While Christmas is a great experience for everyone who takes part in it, sex with Jessica Alba would mostly only be great for me, and me alone. I wouldn't want to share the experience with anyone, especially if you're a dude, so it really wouldn't be that great for everybody the way Christmas is. And I can promise you that there's one person it would *not* be great for, and that's Jessica Alba. So let's give Point A squarely to Christmas.

At Christmas you can always find me either under the mistletoe, or a camel toe! oh!

Point B: Suppose by some freakish twist of fate, I were to have sex with Jessica Alba. Unlike the miracle of Christmas, I'm pretty sure that nobody would choose to celebrate this miracle by giving me presents. You wouldn't even think of it, would you? No, nothing about me getting it on with the hot stripper from *Sin City* is going to affect anybody's spirit of giving. So, when the sex was over, I'd get nothing. Not even the sandwich that I always need after sex, and would no doubt demand that Jessica get up and make me because she's a girl. The promise of no presents and an empty stomach puts Point B also in the festive hands of Christmas.

Point C: When kept in our hearts and minds, the joy and the spirit of the Christmas season can last throughout the whole year. But believe me when I tell you—for me, sex with Jessica Alba would last all of nine seconds. Need I go on? Christmas wins! There's simply nothing better in our whole wide, mixed-up world.

That being said, I've noticed something lately that's a little disturbing to me. And no, it isn't that black midget downtown who has no arms or legs but he has a boom box, and he puts on electronic music and dances "the Worm" for spare change. Although he is very disturbing. And I know he's one of God's creatures and I should embrace him, but I can't lie, the guy just sort of makes me throw up into my own cheeks a little bit, and in my heart I'm mad at him for not just staying home. But even more upsetting than that, to me, is the fact that these days, people seem to have forgotten how to enjoy the holiday season. I know times are more complicated than they've ever been. Everybody's all running around, plugged into their stupid cell phones, and iPods and eBays, and BooBerries, and a lot of other cool stuff that I can't figure out how to use. People are all angry and divided up—Red State vs. Blue State, Have vs. Have Not, Spy vs. Spy, Kramer vs. Black People. The rich are richer, the poor are still getting boned, and the middle class is shrinking up more than my penis did when I saw Debbie Gibson naked in *Playboy*. Hell, we hardly even get snow at Christmas anymore since Al Gore invented global warming as an angry response to something that happened to him down at Disney World. Jeb Bush gave him a wedgie or something—I don't know. I don't read the papers.

You think all this good will and cheer falls out of the sky? It doesn't! It falls out of my holly jolly butt!

But I do know this—at this most festive time of year, when everyone should just sing and dance, and pour some eggnog down their pants, it seems that people all around me are busy, stressful, and uptight. It's as if most people nowadays have lost their holiday spirit. Maybe that's how *you* feel. Maybe that's why you bought this book and took it home. And, I will say at this time, you damn well better have bought this book, because if you are still standing in the store reading this, so help me God, I will come down there and squeeze your head like a freakin' pimple. But if you are at home and feeling like you've lost your holiday spirit, then fear not. Because I have good news, or "tidings," whatever the hell they are. In the spirit of the season, I am here to remind you about how totally wicked-awesome the holidays are. And even better, I will get us all back into the holiday spirit, so we can let the good times roll. I am the perfect man for this job.

Around Quahog, I am known not only as a snappy dresser and a bad father, but also as a self-appointed expert on all things Christmas, as well as a self-described "Huge-O-Naut." "Don't know what that means," says you? Well, let's take one thing at a time, okay, little britches? Just take my hand, follow my lead, and with my help, I boldly promise you that just as surely as fat chicks will often simply splash on more perfume rather than wash themselves, or at least their stinky armpits, which causes their flabby bodies to emit a thick and balmy aroma like that of a big, teeming, steaming bowl of some kind of floral onion soup, so rancid it'll make your eyes water even from three work stations away down at your office—that you and I will have the greatest freakin' holiday season ever. So let's get started!

Peter Griffin

Holiday fun fact: "Missile-toe" was also the locker-room nickname of NFL place kicker Morten Anderson.

Part
One

The
Holiday
Season

# Christmas:
## What the Hell Is It?

**Everybody** knows all about the good stuff that comes with the holiday season—the presents, the food, the family, the laughter, that time I made out with my hot cousin on the coat pile at my uncle Billy's house and even copped a feel. That was so freakin' sweet. I'm sure you have plenty of memorable and mildly disturbing holiday memories of your own. Yes, we all know the special joys of the season. However, not many of us know how it all got started. What the hell is Christmas anyway? Where did it come from, and what is its secret? I sure as hell don't know. And the more I think about it, the more confusing it gets. Years ago, when I was a young boy growing up in Quahog, I never once questioned the true meaning of Christmas—partly because I had yet to lose the childlike sense of wonder that helps make the season so merry and wonderful, but mainly because I went to Catholic school and was savagely beaten by nuns if I ever questioned anything, let alone the birth of our lord and savior, Jesus Christ. Those crazy old women got away with murder. And they could have really, because they knew that they already had a free ticket into heaven as a result of being on the Nun Plan. They were like the bad guy in *Lethal Weapon 2*, only nobody ever showed up and revoked their diplomatic immunity and shot them. And though they claimed to be imbued with the joy and spirit of God's great love and kindness, they sure didn't miss a chance to open an almighty can of whoop-ass on me and my little school chums for any offense, real or imagined. One time they beat me like a rented mule for asking if I could take a leak during a spelling bee. And then, moments later, I took another beating for peeing my pants while writhing on the floor in pain during a spelling bee. Normally, I would've been embarrassed to have peed myself in front of my classmates, but in this case I was actually happy to have urine pouring out of me. Because on that day I had taken some body shots from those brides of Christ that would've put Floyd Patterson on the ropes. And though as a third-grader I didn't quite have a thorough understanding of the human body and all of its functions, in my heart I was certain that the nuns had ruptured my spleen and I was in fact bleeding out through my penis. So given that rough start, rather than ask questions, through the years I learned to piece together things for myself. For quite some time it was my understanding that Christmas was the day that Jesus rose from the dead to feed on the flesh of the living, and so we sing Christmas carols to lull him back to sleep. I thought this for years, until my wife, Lois, sweetly pointed out that I had confused Jesus with former Ugandan dictator Idi Amin, and a flesh-eating zombie from some Roger Corman film I had fallen asleep watching when we were on vacation in New Hampshire. It was only then that I realized I had to revisit the topic and today I find myself more confused than ever.

There are so many things about Christmas that are hard to understand.

If Jesus was born in the desert, what's with all the snow?

For example, what's a Yule log? Huh? You tell me, 'cause I sure as hell
don't know. You say "Yule log" to me, and the only thing I can conjure
up is that it's something that the bald guy from *The King and I* leaves in
the toilet. And I know it isn't that, because who would want that in his
house at any time—let alone around the holidays? Why a Christmas tree?
Or mistletoe? What the hell is mistletoe? And while we're at it, what the
hell is myrrh? And if Jesus was born in the desert, what's with all the
snow? And why would anyone give "twelve lords a-leaping" as a gift?
How would you wrap a lord a-leaping? Wouldn't he be all kicking his legs
and thrashing around? I would. If somebody tried to wrap me up in a box,
you'd better believe I'd kick his ass from hell to breakfast.

Whew! It's no wonder the true meaning of Christmas is forgotten—
there's too much crap to know and remember in the first place! And on
top of that, we all have to learn and respect all the
other holidays that are bundled up with Christmas, which was never the case when I was a
kid. For example, there's Hanukkah, when
our Jewish friends light a candelabra, and
spin a bunch of tops, and sing songs from
*Fiddler on the Roof*. They thank God
for helping them invent Hollywood,

According to tradition, Jewish kids get eight days of presents—one for each of the reindeer on Santa's sleigh. Lucky!

and then pay tribute to some old guy who had a day's worth of oil and it lasted eight days. It's a joyful time and a source of great pride, because as I understand it, this was the very first time in recorded history that a Jewish guy learned how to stretch a buck, a skill that has served them well for many a Christmas season. And then there's Kwanzaa, when our African-American neighbors dress up like Jim Brown on *The Mike Douglas Show* for a celebration of family and culture that to my knowledge, dates back to the release of Paul Simon's *Graceland* album in 1985. Because I swear to God, I never heard of it before then. But irregardless, Lois and I will stop by my friend Cleveland's house to bring him an ear of corn, or a bean pie, or whatever will keep him from thinking I'm the racist that I was brought up to be.

There's also something called winter solstice, which is, I think, celebrated by old pot-smoking hippies and people who listen to public radio. Then there's something called Boxing Day, which is celebrated in Canada. Now, normally I would tell you that I could give a rat's ass about this, because to be honest, I've never cared for Canadians, with the absolute exceptions of Bobby Orr and John Candy. But at Christmastime, I put that attitude away, and that, Little Beaver, is the first step toward getting back your holiday spirit. You see, some people want to use this time of year to divide people up and fan the flames of hatred and indifference. Well, the way I see it, we've got all year to do that. But at Christmastime there's room for everyone at the table—and the more the merrier! It's like in *The Grinch*, when he sat down to carve the roast beast. Think about it . . . there were a butt-load of Whos at that table, of all shapes and sizes. And you know most of them probably didn't worship a proper lord. But so what? They all got a slice of roast beast, and they all got along and had one hell of a time together. They even knew all the words to that happy "Da-who door-ayes" song, which even after forty years of viewing are still as elusive to me as the lyrics to "Inna-Gadda-Da-Vida."

My point, Your Honor, is simply that if those rhyming, fictional, little cartoon circus freaks can get it together for the holidays, then so can we! It's an ideal that was summed up perfectly by my cousin Alan one time when we were both drunk off our asses on the golf course. He said to me, "Y'know, Peter, between you and me, I don't like you that much. You're a fat, stupid lump of dirt. But, hey, it doesn't mean we can't have a good time together." And he was right! So Happy Kwanzaa-Hanukkah-Solstice-Pagan Ritual-Boxing-New Year's-Cool-Yule-Navidad-Katilsday, everyone! Let's have some fun together at least once a year, no matter what we call it or where it came from. Let go and accept everyone, and I promise you, you're gonna feel better.

But just so you know, I am gonna say "Christmas" a lot instead of "Holidays," so just hang with me on that and don't get a bug up your ass when it happens. I can't help it. To me it's still the granddaddy of all holidays. And I'm not alone! Hell, even Irving Berlin was dreaming of a "White Christmas," and you know he didn't go to Catholic school! What a gift he gave us all for Christmas—and he was a Jew! Come to think of it, so was Jesus. And Amy Irving, which to this day absolutely staggers me. But again, let's not worry about that now. Because I'm gonna fill your heart with so much love, joy, and inner peace that you'll get all blissed out and spiritual, and maybe even turn your back on the material world. And then you'll grow a big beard and embrace peace so much that you'll start to look like a crazed religious fanatic that nobody wants to see or hear from, let alone sit next to on an airplane. Just like Cat Stevens. And if that happens, I will be the first one to call the authorities and have your peace-loving ass sent straight to Gitmo. But until then, you and I are gonna have a great holiday. I know this is true. Even if I still don't know what the hell a Yule log is.

# The Holiday Season: "Holy Crap! Already!?!"

**One time** when I was a kid, I was watching *Donny and Marie*. It was their special Christmas episode and all the Osmonds were there. They were all wearing sweaters and scarves, and a bunch of gay people were ice-skating around on that fake ice of theirs. Marie had some kind of old-fashioned bonnet on her head with a long coat, and she had both hands stuffed into a big furry muff. And as fake snow flew through the air, everyone was singing that song, "It's Beginning to Look a Lot Like Christmas." My mother said it was a beautiful vision of a Christmas scene, and it probably was. But at twelve years old, there was only one vision that I could focus on, and that was Marie Osmond with both of her fists buried deep in a big furry muff.

That was one freakin' sweet Christmas vision I will always savor—and just one in a series of embarrassing impromptu and unwanted erections that poked out of my pajamas in full view of my mother and various and sundry houseguests and relatives through the years.

Well, every year I'm reminded of that scene when the first signs of Christmas decorations appear here in

> Jingles Bells, Batman smells, Robin laid an egg... Batmobile lost its wheel... and, uh...I forget the words.

Quahog and the whole damn town starts to "look a lot like Christmas." The problem nowadays is that this usually starts to happen about a week and a half after Labor Day. Sometime in early to mid-September, all the Halloween stuff down at the Quahog Pharmacy is actually looking over its shoulders at all the Christmas stuff that's bullying its way onto the shelves behind it. To this I say, "Hey, Madison Avenue . . . what's the freakin' hurry? I mean, come on! Chris and I are barely done trick-or-treating and you're already cramming Christmas down our throats? Take a pill, will you?" Oh, by the way, here's a tip—next Halloween, buy *two* costumes. That way, you can cover the whole neighborhood, go home, change into the second costume, hit every house again . . . and, Bam! Double candy! Okay, I should have saved this tip, but I thought it would be a good sneak preview for my next book, *Peter Griffin's Guide to Halloween*, which I am now certain will happen, since this book is going so well, don't you think?

 *Visit www.harpercollins.com for more information about this book and others by the Griffin clan.

You know, they tell you to "shop until you drop," but the last time I did that they made me clean it up and I was permanently banned from the store.

Anyway, if you are gonna get two costumes, you'd better hurry. Because I kid you not, in no time, all the costumes will be replaced with Christmas crap—cheesy plastic wreaths and white wire-mesh reindeers and those big inflatable snow globes with a fan in them that blows fake snow around inside, like the one I wasted a hundred bucks on last Christmas. It took me two hours and I nearly popped a vein in my head blowing that thing up with my mouth. Then it worked for about an hour—just long enough for my neighbor Quagmire to tell me how stupid it looked—and then it sprung a leak and ended up all flat and sad-looking on my yard like a giant, used, colorful Fiesta condom. In fact, every yard on Spooner Street was littered with those stupid deflated snow globes last year. Well, except for Quagmire's yard, which is always littered with actual condoms. And then, what do you do with that thing? You can't just throw it out—it cost a hundred bucks! So you tell yourself that you'll fix it, but you never do. Mine is still outside, all dirty and draped halfway over our picnic table. This is just one of the little things that make people say, "You know what? Christmas is crap! The hell with it!" And you know what? Every year, for a little while—I agree with them!

I mean, think about it. It's all too freakin' much. In fact, "It grinds my gears!" (Thank you. Thank you, very much.) First of all, look at how much money we spend on Christmas. And did you know that when you use a credit card, at the end of the month they send you a bill? And you have to pay it? What the hell kind of bargain is that? It's pointless even to have one of those things, and yet I make the same mistake every year. And remarkably, every Christmas they send me a *new* credit card, just in time for me to get caught up in that same tangled web, which, in the spirit of the season, I do. Man! As the great, though never funny, Yakov Smirnoff used to say, "What a country!" By the way, last summer I got an awesome Boston Red Sox credit card, and when I signed up for it, they gave me a free Red Sox beach towel. A few weeks ago, my friend Max Weinstein told me that so far, that beach towel has cost me over six thousand dollars in interest payments. And you know what? It was worth every penny. Go Sox! Yankees suck! Yeah!

Christmas shopping. Is there anything worse than that annual tragic human stampede? We hit the malls loaded with nothing but questions and anxiety. What to buy? How old are my kids now? I have *kids*? How did that happen? She told me she would pull out! Well, that's a woman for you! Okay, so what should I buy these kids of mine? What is hip to them anymore? What toys are in this year? Why every year do they create a Christmas gift that everybody has to have, but then they don't make enough of them for all of us to buy? Like, one year, it was Tickle Me Elmo,

or Touch Me Inappropriately Ernie, or something, and everybody wanted them, but nobody had them! Last year it was Xbox 9000 or some other dumb-ass thing that would be obsolete by February—when the shelves would be packed with them, by the way—and isn't *that* a black fly in my chardonnay? And some guys actually got shot waiting in line for one of these things, which is, in my opinion, simply asinine. Yes, "asinine" is the perfect word to use here. I say that not only because it has the word "ass" in it, but also because as crazy as it all gets, I would never go so far as to shoot anyone at Christmas—not even the guy who made that "Jingle Bells" record with the Singing Dogs. I might rough him up a little just to make him think about it next time, but shoot him? No way.

And most of us wouldn't. Instead, we collapse under the stress and the pressure of it all. We get the flu, or a sinus infection, or go absolutely berserk and have a psychotic break down, like my wife, Lois, did just a few

Christmases ago. She really lost it and went on a rampage until my neighbor Joe shot her down from the giant tree in the center of town with the same kind of tranquilizer dart that game wardens use to bring down bull elephants, or that the police used to stop James Brown years ago when he was racing through Atlanta high on PCP and firing a pistol out the window of his car. Lois would later tell me that her anger was triggered by something about how people should be accountable for their own joy at Christmas, instead of passively sitting back and waiting for it to be created for them. But you and I know both know that there was really only one reason for her behavior, which was that she was menstruating. And this, my fellow Americans, is why we will never elect a woman president.

So where does all this leave us? I guess it leaves us feeling pretty crappy, huh? Kind of right where we started, back in the bookstore—completely lost in the hustle and bustle of the holiday season. Well, buck up there, sports fans. Because if there's anything that Christmas teaches us, it's that anyone who is lost can be found. Well, anyone except for the people on the TV show *Lost*, but don't even get me started on that piece of crap. No, I'd rather talk about another TV show. One that only comes on once a year at Christmastime and was written by one of your all-time wicked good writers, Mr. Charles Dickens. I know . . . let's just take a minute. *Dickens.* Can you believe that? The guy's last name was *Dickens*! Oh my God, I practically bust a nut just thinking about it. Oh! Oh, that reminds me—we used to play softball against a team from a town on Cape Cod called Yarmouth. And get this, the team was sponsored by a restaurant there called Dick's Inn. Honest to God. Their uniforms actually said, "Dick's Inn, Yarmouth." I also heard there was a guy from Holden, Massachusetts, called Richard Hertz, and he was always introduced as "Dick Hertz from Holden," which is so perfect that it has to be made up. But anyway, the Dick we're talking about isn't from Massachusetts. I think he lives in France and he's written a crap-load of books when he's not eating

cheese and wine and going "Oh-ho-ho," like LeBeau on *Hogan's Heroes*, and making an A-OK sign and winking so he looks like a cartoon chef on a pizza box, which is what most people do in France. And even though I've never read any of his books, there's one story he wrote that I know by heart. It's a holiday classic for all ages, and Charles Dickens's greatest piece of writing. Of course, I'm talking about *Mister Magoo's Christmas Carol*, starring Jim Backus. It's a great story with some catchy songs, period costumes, scary ghosts, and some partial nudity, which was not included in the original telecast but I have since added in my mind. Jim Backus is so good as Mr. Magoo in this that you would swear you were actually watching Mr. Magoo. And the message of his spooky Christmas adventure is as fresh today as it was when Dickens first wrote it back in the golden age of vaudeville, when it was performed twelve times a day, with special matinee performances on Wednesdays and Saturdays.

And I promise you that by tracing the steps of Mr. Magoo's journey, you and I will find our way back to the magic and wonder of Christmas. Oooooh! Isn't this going to be fun? Look! I think I see our first ghost already! It's Bette Davis, star of the silver screen, and she's saying, "Booo-oooo! Fasten your seatbelts—it's going to be a bumpy night!" And look over there! It's legendary comic performer John Belushi! And he's saying, "Booo-oooo! On the short list of positives about being dead, is the fact that I never, ever have to watch my brother's truly horrible sitcom, *According to Jim*. Wow! We've learned something already, and we're not even into part two!

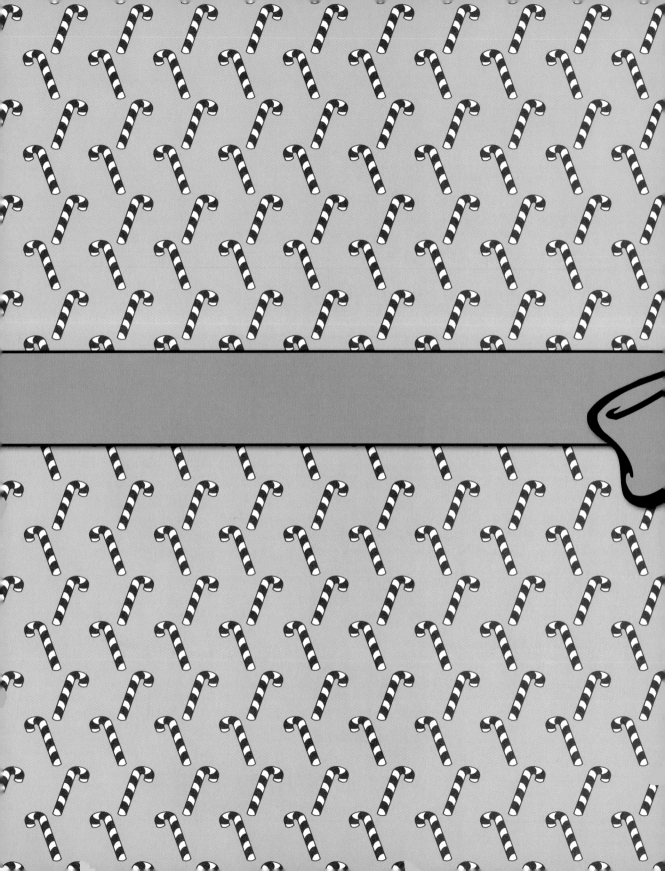

Part
Two

Christmas
Past

**Okay,** so we're following Mr. Magoo's story, and you can skip all the crap about Bob Cratchit and his little crippled kid because he's going to be fine. They jerk you around, making you think he's gonna die and all that, but he doesn't. In fact, he'll probably get better enough to be able to go to Disney World, but still have a wheelchair, and you know what that means. That's right, it means he's gonna get to cut the lines, the little pecker. I hate that. Crippled people have all the luck. And even worse are those morbidly obese people who rent wheelchairs 'cause they're too fat to lumber around that place. Like me, you're probably saying, "Why should *they* be able to cut the line? How come I have to wait for three hours to see Mr. Toad, and that wide-load doesn't?" Well, I know why, because I got into a shoving match with some fat-ass broad over this the last time I was down there. And later, when I was being escorted out of the Magic Kingdom and into the custody of the Orlando Police Department, I was informed that the whole "wheelchair courtesy" is a stated policy of Disney World. Well, I think it's time we state a new policy, which is simply this—if you're too fat to walk, you don't get to go to Disney World. Screw Disney, anyway! For my money, they haven't done anything good since the 1970s Mickey Mouse Club, which featured

a young Lisa Whelchel, who went on to play Blair on the *Facts of Life*, and who these days could tell you more than I ever could about Jesus—whether you like it or not—and who, like most of the *Facts of Life* girls, could also probably tell you a thing or two about tooling around Disney World in a wheelchair. But anyway, back to Christmas.

So in the night, Mr. Magoo is visited by three ghosts, and the first one is the Ghost of Christmas Past. Now, trust me, if this ever happens to you—and I really hope it doesn't, because for the most part, ghosts showing up is never a very good thing. I mean, look at *Poltergeist*. So many bad things happened to the family in that movie, and they kept on happening, even when it was done. Just about every person who was in that movie is now dead. Well, except of course for Craig T. Nelson, but patience. Patience. And what about that movie *Ghost*? My God, you could end up like Demi Moore, crying thick, fake glycerin tears while throwing a pot with Patrick Swayze to a spooky old Righteous Brothers song. Yeesh, I shudder just thinking about it. Get your icy fingers off me, Swayze! Go haunt a dance studio somewhere, you handsome, limber fruit! Anyway, I hope none of these things happen to you, but trust me, if the Ghost of Christmas Past shows up, just touch his robe and take that ride. Believe me when I tell ya, this is definitely the ghost you want to take a trip with. Because I have seen this story told a million times with a lot of different people in the Mr. Magoo part. And no matter who it is—Mickey Mouse, Kermit the Frog, the guy who played Patton, even Frasier, I think, played Mr. Magoo—but no matter who it was, the Ghost of Christmas Past always showed them a good time. And how could he not? There's something about the past that always seems more magical when we look back.

I know that Christmas was always the best time of the year when I was a kid, and not only because the rest of the year really sucked for me, which I'm sure it did. But, still I would travel back to any of it in a heartbeat, because time, and years of seriously dangerous binge-drinking, have erased almost all of the memories of sadness, and of despair, and of calling Child Services in the night to please, *please* send someone by to keep my uncle Roy out of my room. Yes, time has a way of healing all wounds. And it's a good thing, because without this phenomenon, my son Stewie would never have been born. You see, my son Chris weighed twenty-six pounds at birth. And upon delivery, he split my wife, Lois, open like a ripe summer melon. She vowed never to go through such a thing again.

But that ol' devil time took care of that, and today I have two beautiful children. And Meg. And my children will no doubt share many happy Christmas memories. The kind that I had as a small boy growing up in Quahog.

I saw Mommy kissing Santa Claus... only he didn't have a red suit or a beard, and he was my Uncle Roy.

# Christmas as a Kid: Always Awesome

**Ah yes . . .** "Christmas Past." Of all the memories I can savor in this big fat life of mine, nothing makes me happier than looking back at the joy and excitement of Christmas Eve. I remember leaving milk and cookies out for Santa. Brushing my teeth. Putting on my warm, red flannel feety-pajamas. Then checking the sky for reindeer before saying my prayers, snuggling under the covers, and trying with all my might to go to sleep.

And hours later, in the magical predawn light of another Christmas morning, I remember waking up in a cold, soggy puddle, my pajamas soaked, and the air reeking with a pungent ammonia smell as I realized that once again I had wet the bed in excited anticipation of Santa's big arrival. I remember this particular Christmas moment with vivid clarity, because it was just last year. But looking back, as we are now, I realize that the same thing happened almost

Dear Santa,
Please leave me lots of toys, and if possible, do something to take Zach Braff down a few pegs.

every Christmas Eve when I was a boy. And how could it not? There's simply nothing more exciting for a kid than that special night. Your heart is pounding, your eyes are wide with awe and amazement . . . it's the closest thing to having sex that children can experience, only they don't know this at the time because most young children have never had sex, unless they're Tatum O'Neal or whoever Roman Polanski is dating this year.

Santa Claus—what a guy, huh? I remember flying down the stairs on Christmas morning and seeing all of my presents wrapped under the tree. Tearing open the brightly colored boxes to find a G.I. Joe with life-like hair, a Fonzie doll with "thumbs-up" action, or an official Red Ryder BB Gun with a compass in the stock and this thing that tells the time. Now, I know, you think I'm just quoting Ralphie from *A Christmas Story* here, but I really did get a BB gun one Christmas. And yes, thank you for your concern, but no, I did *not* shoot my eye out! I did however shoot my neighbor's eye out. And it was really awful. But in my defense I was trying to shoot his cat, which I was at the time pretending was not a cat, but a big-game Bengal tiger who was stalking our home. It's not my fault that my neighbor came out to pick the cat up just as I was drawing a bead on him. His name was Frank McGurk, and for somebody who fought in the Korean War, he sure screamed like a girl when that BB hit him in the eye. Thankfully, his veteran's benefits paid for most of his medical expenses, but he still sued my parents for pain and suffering. He tried to get everything they owned but ended up settling for my father's red Plymouth Valiant, and for a long time after that my dad had to take the bus to work. Boy did I love that gun! I always loved everything Santa brought me when I was a kid. Well, except that one Christmas when I was in the fourth grade. I went down to the Outlet department store in Providence with my folks to see Santa. I sat on his lap and asked him to bring me a bike that I had picked out of the Sears Christmas catalog. It was green with butterfly handlebars and a banana seat with a "sissy bar" on the

back, which made it easy to pop wheelies. I knew if I had that bike I could ride it to school and I'd look just like Peter Fonda in *Easy Rider*. And I'd sing the guitar part to "Born to Be Wild" and all the girls in my class would look at me. Sweet. Now, I don't know if the Santa at the Outlet was just having an off night, or if maybe he wasn't listening as much. And I don't know if it hurt my chances of getting that green bike, but I had eaten a whole box of Pillsbury Space Food Sticks that afternoon, and when I got up on Santa's lap, I ripped a really bad fried egg–smelling fart that burned my butt and the part of his thigh that I was sitting on. I tried to pretend it didn't happen and quickly told Santa all about the cool bike I wanted. But he just looked at me for a minute and then, in a thick North Providence accent, just said, "Ah, God dammit! What the hell's wrong with you, kid?"

I guess that should have tipped me off that something had gone really, really wrong. And it had. Because when I came downstairs that Christmas morning, I looked under the tree and I *did* see a brand-new bike. But it wasn't the bike I had asked Santa for. Yes, it had butterfly handle bars, but they had white sparkly tassels hanging from them. And yes, it had the banana seat and the sissy bar, but it didn't have the normal bar that goes from the seat to the front wheel. And guess what? It wasn't green like I asked for. It was pink! And you know why? Because it was a freakin' girl's bike! Santa Claus brought me a girl's bike! It looked just like the bike that Jan Brady was riding when she crashed into the family portrait they were hiding in the garage because she wasn't wearing her glasses. I was dumbfounded, and I tried really hard not to cry. My mother stood there with a cigarette hanging out of her mouth and said, "What? What's your problem?" And I said, "It's pink." She shrugged and puffed a drag off the butt she was smoking, and said, "Yeah. So what? Pink is mod. Like on *Rowan and Martin's Laugh-In*. That's a very mod bike." And I tried to say, "But it's a girl's bike," but the only thing that came out of my throat was air, and a tiny squeaking noise where the word "girl" was supposed to be.

And that's when all hell broke loose. My father screamed at me and called me a spoiled, ungrateful child before storming off to work at the mill. My father worked every Christmas, by the way. Good times. My mother agreed with him, and told me there were millions of children in China who would love to have a bike like this but never would. And I knew this was complete bull, because I'd seen pictures of China on TV and if there's one thing that everybody in China has, it's a bike. In fact, that's the only thing they have in China besides chopsticks and fireworks. I knew I couldn't argue this with my mother, so I decided to make the best of it. On the first day I tried riding that bike to school, I put baseball cards in the spokes to make it sound more like a motorcycle. But as I went flapping into that schoolyard, I knew

I looked nothing like Peter Fonda from *Easy Rider*. Instead I'm pretty sure I looked like Penelope Pitstop from the *Wacky Races*. And the girls did look at me as I arrived. But while I was hoping they'd be impressed somehow, they all just pointed and laughed at me. Well, all of them except this big bull-dikey chick from the fifth grade named Mary-Lou Donato. She did not laugh. She just called me a "pickle-smoocher" and knocked me off my bike onto the cement. Later on, when I was holding ice on my head in the school nurse's office, Sister Mary Evelyn suggested that maybe Mary-Lou was jealous of the lovely bicycle that Santa Claus had brought me. Well, if that were the case, I would've gladly let her take it home just to get rid of it. I hated that bike. I even left it overnight out in front of the Cumberland Farms convenient store, in the hopes that some bad kids would steal it, but nobody did. Bad boys don't want to be seen riding a girl's bike, and girls don't steal bikes, so I was stuck with it. And all because I farted on Santa at the Outlet Company.

But then, one day, that Christmas magic took over. I was at school and I thought about what Santa Claus himself had said to me: "God dammit! What's the hell's wrong with you, kid?" His wise words repeated in my brain until I thought, "Yeah. What the hell is wrong with me?" Sure, that bike was pink and I looked like a real fruitcake riding it. But if Santa gave it to me—or my parents did—maybe it was the only bike left in his workshop—or the only one they could afford.

And sure, maybe somebody gave me a really bad bike. But at least they thought enough of me to give me one at all. And maybe they didn't even know how bad the bike was. I mean, Santa and my parents were really, really old. Old people don't know when something looks horrible. Did you ever see how most of them dress to go to the Hometown Buffet? Santa was right. Something *was* wrong with me. And maybe I *was* a spoiled, ungrateful little child after all. Well, let me tell you, something happened to me that day. Like when the Grinch's heart grew three sizes up on Mount Crumpet. Something changed. And I decided I was gonna go home and ride that pink bike no matter how much it made me look like a young fat Charles Nelson Reilly at a street fair. I would ride that bike every day to show my parents and Santa just how much I truly appreciated everything they ever did for me. It was the "Christmas spirit" that filled me up that day. And it lightened my steps all the way home . . . until I arrived at my house and found that my mother was having a yard sale and had already sold my bike for a quarter. And this was the greatest Christmas miracle of all. Because I truly hated that freakin' bike. I hated it like poison.

# Christmas Dinner: "Get Out Those Folding Chairs!"

**On Christmas** day, around noon, I would stare in wonder at the tree. The floor around it was littered with empty boxes and crumpled up wrapping paper, and all of my new toys, which were already broken and worthless. I would reflect on the thrill of the morning, still trying to catch my breath as I stood wearily, with sad, errant peel-and-stick bows haphazardly clinging to my shins and the ass part of my pajamas. And it was always at this happy moment that my mother would storm in from the kitchen and sternly caution me to "not get comfortable." With my father already gone to work a twelve-hour shift at the mill—and again, thanks a bundle for that, Dad—it was left to me to help my mother get the house ready for the family dinner she prepared for no less than thirty or forty of our drunk Irish relatives. And every year as I was setting the table, I would smack my lips and dream of a golden-brown Butterball turkey, cooked to perfection and surrounded by creamy mashed potatoes and emerald-green peas. Mmmmm . . . it was a beautiful dream, and a pointless dream because my mother—like most Irish women—was a truly horrible cook. Every meal in my house growing up was either burned black or boiled white. And on Christmas, it didn't help that by noon, my mother was usually already halfway into a bottle of what she called her "cooking sherry," but which was, in fact, a screw-top bottle of Boone's Farm Strawberry Hill jug wine.

My dinner place back then was out in the sun porch at the kids' table, just as it has been for the last forty-two years. It's funny how even now, I still don't get to sit at the big table, in spite of the fact that most of the grown-ups are dead or suffering horribly in a home somewhere. But ah, I can still see those happy faces, jolly as ever, and hear the din of their sweet Irish voices still booming with great joy, holiday spirit, and a barely concealed rage born out of hundreds of years of oppression at the hands of the British. "Merry Chrish-mish to all of ush!" my uncle Mike would say, his eyes already at half-mast, and his Flintstone glass of Carling Black Label held high, to which his wife, my auntie Alice, would reply, "Sit down, Mike, you're making an ass of yourself, you pickle-eyed mutt." And Uncle Mike would tell her to shut up and say that he's oh so sorry that he can't be more like her precious Jack Kennedy. And this would start my auntie Mary on her annual rant about the Kennedys' being the closest thing that we've ever had to royalty in

Merry Chrish-mish to all of ush!

this country, which would make my uncle Dave call her nothing but a royal pain in the ass.

And Aunt Mary would tell Uncle Dave that if she wanted any crap out of him, she would squeeze his head. Then my auntie Bea would suggest that perhaps some of them had had too much to drink, to which my cousin Dennis would yell that he needed gallons of liquid to wash down the dry hunks of shoe leather that my mom tried to pass off as turkey every year. This always brought uncle Roy to his feet in defense of my mother's cooking, which was never a good thing because it always drew attention to the one thing that nobody ever really wanted to talk about, which was that my uncle Roy wasn't really my uncle and that he only came around my house when my father was at work, which was always. Before long the first punch would be thrown, usually by my cousin Pat, and the table that I had taken such care in setting would be flipped over. Then, sweeter than the bells of Saint Mary's, the air would be filled with the sounds of breaking glass, screaming, and profanity that have always said "Christmas" to me.

Eventually, a fuse would blow, as it did every year, since every light in the house was on, as well as the TV, the Chrismas tree, and my mother's old phonograph, which repeatedly played Side One of Mitch Miller's *Holiday Sing Along with Mitch* album. The house would be shrouded in darkness and for a brief moment we would all get to experience the "Silent Night" that we've so often heard celebrated in song. The silence would be soon broken by the soft weeping of my aunt Edna, the passing of gas from any or all who were there, and the swearing as my uncle Pee-Wee would fall down the basement stairs as he went to change the fuse. Soon the coats would go on and my big happy family would head off into the cold winter's night, leaving us with a bagful of memories, a mountain of unwashed and broken dishes, and the solemn vow that none of us would ever speak to each other again. But deep down, we all knew that even if we didn't always see eye to eye, even if we didn't respect our differences and the choices we've made in our lives, even if we didn't really know or like each other at all, really, we'd all be back again next year, sitting around that same happy table, with the possible exception of smelly old Aunt Doris, who we all wished would die already. Isn't that what family is all about? Merry Chrish-mish, everybody!

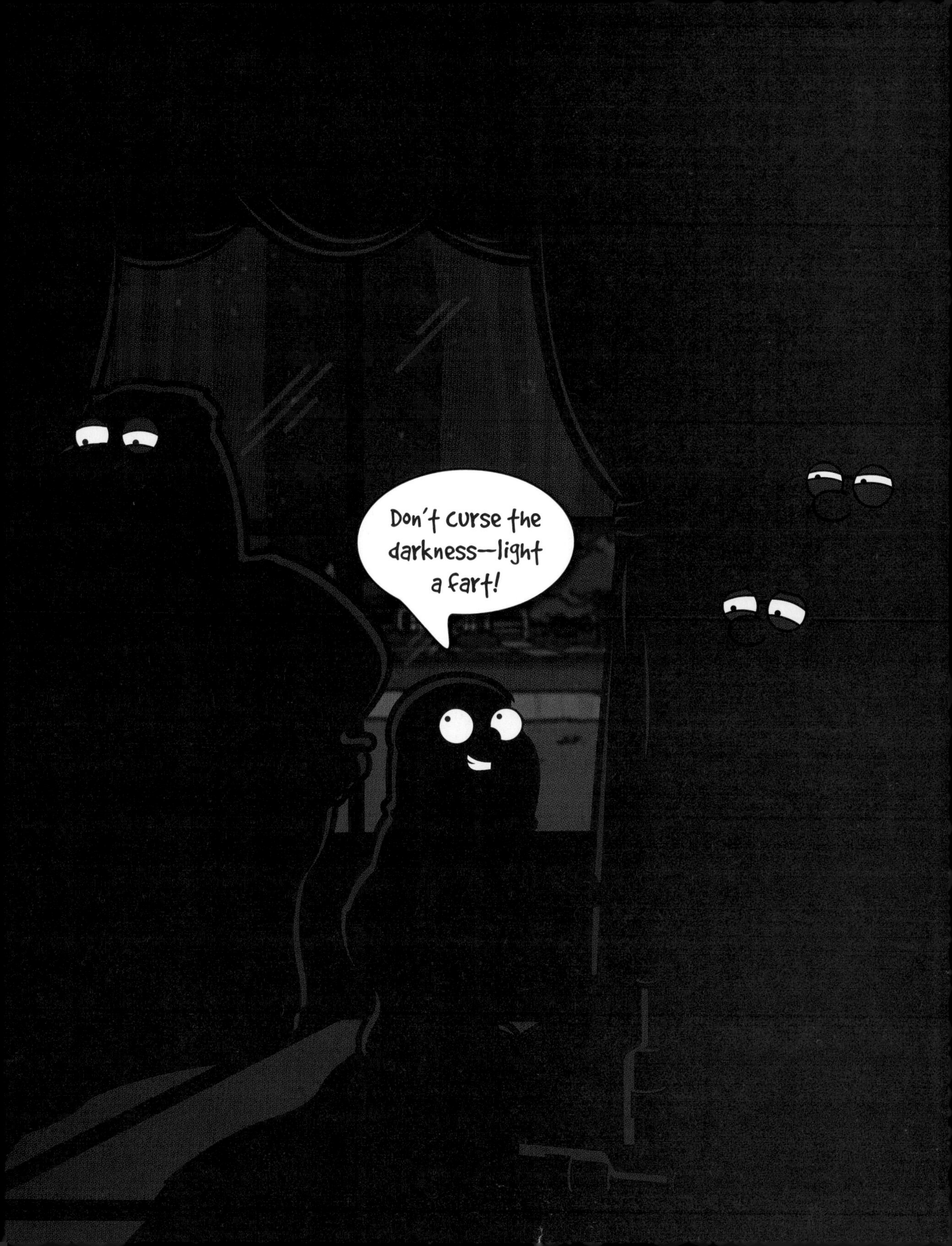
Don't curse the darkness—light a fart!

# The Christmas Tree: Our Brightest Christmas Symbol

**Another** Jewish fingerprint all over our happy holiday season is the Christmas tree, which was invented by a small Jewish man named Moe Tannenbaum, as a thank-you to America for freeing Europe from Castro in World War II. You're welcome, Moe! And thank *you*, sir, for inventing a Christmas symbol that for two weeks of every year would transform my childhood home into a place that looked green and festive and smelled like a beautiful enchanted pine forest, instead of the usual sickening blend of secondhand smoke, my father's BO, and milk products that had gone past their expiration date.

It was always on a snowy night in mid-December that my mom would drag my dad down to the Christmas tree lot in front of the A&W Root Beer stand that was boarded up for the winter. And every year we went through the same routine. Mom would pick out a tree and Dad would ask how much it cost. And the Christmas tree salesman would say, "Fifteen dollars," and my father would say, "Fifteen dollars? Are you out of your mind? For a tree that will be dead in a week? Do you know how hard I have to work to make fifteen dollars? If I were to pay that much for a tree, it had better come with the roots, you thieving Bedouin. And I don't see roots here. In fact, I see nothing here but crooks and willing fools with their hard-earned money. And I will have none of it! I'm going to work!" Then Dad would storm off to the mill on foot, and every year I would panic, thinking this year would finally be the year that I lived in a house without a Christmas tree. But every year my mom would come to the rescue. After a brief standoff, Mom would calmly take the salesman behind the blue Porta-John, where he had his thermos and a small radio playing Christmas music on a wooden crate next to his folding chair. I don't know exactly what kind of Christmas magic my mom weaved behind that Porta-John, but within minutes, we were driving back to our house, a tall Douglas fir strapped to the roof of our car, and my mother at the wheel, slowly puffing on a Kent cigarette while staring through the windshield at the winter snow with cold, lifeless eyes.

No matter what tree we ended up with, it was always about two feet too tall for our living room, so every year we would make two new sets of scratch marks on the ceiling in there. We'd make one set of scratch marks when we stood the tree up and another when we pulled it back down to hack the top of it off with a Ginsu knife, because my father's good saw was rusted over since I had left it out in the yard years earlier when trying in vain to build a go-cart. And all of this happened only after hours of grunting and struggling with that stupid wrought-iron tree stand with the three big bolts that never really stood the tree up straight and would always leave my mother bathed in sweat and cursing Christmas, my father, and the day that I was born. Our tree-cutting—or "trimming," as the Pilgrims called it—always left a big fat ugly spot on the top, so our tree always looked less like the lovely triangular models you've seen on Christmas cards and more like a short, pudgy, angry wax museum replica of deceased Chicago mayor Richard Daley wearing a fuzzy green sweater.

All of that soon changed, though, when Mom and I would transform our little tree by decorating it with tinsel and colorful "bubble-lights" from Benny's Home and Auto, and the dozens of beautiful glass ornaments that had been in my mother's family for years. As long as I live, I will never forget those lights, that tinsel, and the back-handers I endured every year after breaking some of those beautiful glass ornaments that had been in my mother's family for years. Yes, every year there were more empty spaces in the ornament boxes, which Mom didn't always discover until we took the tree down on New Year's Day—or, I guess I should say, when *I* took the tree down while Mom would just lay there on the couch nursing a hangover that in her words "would kill God."

No, it wasn't perfect, but still, it was always fun. I'll tell you one thing that isn't fun, though, and that's a chimney fire. I discovered this on the one year that I was too tired to drag our tree out to the road for Big Trash Day, and I got the bright idea to stuff as much of it into the fireplace as possible and then set it on fire. It seemed to make sense, since wood is what we usually burned in the fireplace—well, wood and all of my KISS albums, which I had to hand over

after somebody put it in my father's head that "KISS" actually stood for "Kids in the Service of Satan." I always thought that was stupid, since those letters would've actually spelled out "KITSOS," which was not the name of the band at all. But my father had that look in his eye, and I knew that if I used the word "stupid" in that moment, I probably would have gone right into that fire, too. Right on top of *Destroyer*, *Hotter Than Hell*, and all the other masterpieces of my Rock n' Roll heroes. In retrospect, for a true KISS fan, that would not have been such a bad way to go, but I almost never made it to that day because of what happened when I tried to burn my Christmas tree in our fireplace. I could only get about a third of the tree into the hearth, and although I had no science to back it up, my theory was that the tree would somehow "burn itself up" into the chimney—sort of like a bottle rocket. But no bottle rocket or any illegal firework I had ever lit up on the Fourth of July would have prepared me for what happened on that day when I set a wooden match to our dried-up old Christmas tree. At first it wouldn't light at all until I remembered to blow on the flame, as I had learned during my brief stint as a Cub Scout.

What happened next was astonishing, as well as horrifying, because within two seconds, the damn thing went up like the *Hindenburg*. The room was filled with the brightest white light I have ever seen—brighter even than the light from the mother ship when those stretchy Pillsbury Dough Boy aliens came out of it in *Close Encounters*. It may have even been briefly beautiful, but unlike all those awe-struck scientists in that movie, I did not have a pair of very cool modern scientist sunglasses. I also did not have an industrial arc welder's mask, which was more of what the situation required. And until late in the month of April that year, I also did not have eyebrows, since they had been singed off by the inferno that was roaring out of our hearth and consuming everything in its path, including my parents' wedding portrait, which had hung above the mantle for years. More frightening than the heat was the sound, which was a combination of an angry lion's roar and an actual 757 passenger jet taking off in my living room. Overall, I can liken the experience to something that has only ever been witnessed by the doomed citizens of Hiroshima and Nagasaki, which I would never wish on any human being at any time, let alone during the holidays. Never again, America. Never again.

At this time I would be remiss if I did not once again thank Captain Thomas DeAngelis of the Quahog Fire Department for pulling me out of the blaze and saving our home, and for reassuring my parents that he sees two or three chimney fires a year at Christmas, which made me seem slightly less brain-dead than they thought. And again, thank *you*, Moe Tannenbaum. When you said, "Our Brightest Christmas Symbol," you weren't just whistling "Dixie"—which I know a Jew would never do.

# Christmas Cookies: I Even Ate the Burned Ones!

**As much** as I truly love the holidays, there are still many time-honored Christmas traditions that I have never experienced. For example, I've never ridden in a one-horse open sleigh or roasted chestnuts on an open fire or ever had anyone bring me a figgy pudding. In fact, I have no idea what the hell a figgy pudding is. But I can tell you for certain that it sounds like something that would taste like crap, and I would probably spit most of it out into my hand if somebody did bring me one. I don't recall ever "laughing all the way" to anywhere—although I do remember laughing all the way home from an Adam Sandler movie. That guy is awesome. "I'm fork-on-my-head boy! I have a fork on my head!" Dammit, I don't know how in the world he comes up with that stuff! Oh . . . just in case you haven't seen that—when he says it, he's holding a fork on his head! So, he *is* fork-on-my-head boy! Get it? Damn, freakin' genius. You know, I'll bet he doesn't even try to make up these things. I'll bet they just come through him, you know? Like Mozart or Van Morrison or Murphy Brown. Boy did she come out with 'em, too! Yeah, that old Murphy Brown was a pepper pot. But how could she not be? Growing up in that house with Jerry Mahoney and all those other Muppets that her father did the

voices for. Anyway, the one Christmas tradition I can tell you a lot about
is the baking of Christmas cookies. Because every year, about a week
before Christmas, my mother would take down an old Rendell plaid metal
lunch box that was loaded with Christmas cookie cutters in the shapes
of bells and Santas and snowmen. And we would put on the Mitch Miller
Christmas record and I would help my mom make Christmas cookies for
all of our friends and neighbors. Now, I know your first thought upon
hearing this is "Gay!" because honestly, that's actually my first
thought, even though it's my own story that I'm telling you.
But you and I would both be wrong here, because making
Christmas cookies was beyond belief one of the best days of
the year for me when I was a kid.

The great thing about Christmas Cookie Day was that
my mother did all the lousy, not-fun stuff, like mixing the
batter and rolling the dough. She was just like that chicken in
the children's story. You know, the one who did all the work to
bake the bread, and nobody would help her, but when the bread
was all baked, all the other animals wanted to eat it and she just
said, "Screw you," and ate all the bread herself? She was like that, only she
didn't eat any of the cookies, I did. And she never said, "Screw you," but
through the years I remember her sobbing softly at the stove, and saying,
"I hate my life." And one time she said, "I wish I had aborted you" just
because I was trying to lick cookie batter off the Hamilton Beach mixer.
In her defense, the mixer was running at the time, and when the metal
beaters cut into my tongue, I bled into a whole bowl of batter, which
meant nobody was getting Snowball cookies on their platter that year. I did,
however, get to eat the whole bowl with a spoon, and when Mom realized
I had done it, she got really sick to her stomach. And that sucked because
whenever she puked, it always made me puke, and then the sight of all

that blood-tainted batter coming out of me started a chain-reaction barf-off between the two of us that went on long into the night.

But don't think it was all bad times, because Mom and I always knew how to find the fun in any tough chore. For instance, one time my mom burned a whole sheet of jolly fat snowman cookies. I scraped five of them off the pan, propped them up on the table, and said, "Look, Ma . . . it's the New York Knicks!" And she didn't get the joke until I explained to her that most of the New York Knicks were really big black guys. She smirked a little, so I tried to make her laugh by making them play basketball for her. I was moving them around, saying, "Willis Reed passes it to Walt Frazier!" And then she got it, because my mother looked off into the distance, nodded, and said that she wished she could someday be alone in a room with five giant black guys. And this really surprised me, because I never knew my mother had any interest at all in basketball. But I will never forget her smile in that moment. It was a warm and dreamy smile—the kind that only happens at Christmas.

Our kitchen table was like a candy store, with dozens of open containers of sprinkles and other candy decorations. Mom would smear white frosting on the cookies, and I would use green sprinkles to make a tree cookie, chocolate sprinkles with a red cinnamon button to make a "Rudolph" cookie, and two Hershey kisses as nipples to make a sultry, "Adrienne Barbeau from *Maude* and *Swamp Thing*" cookie. Mom would do her best to arrange our treats into festive Christmas foil plates, but it wasn't easy for her, because the smell and the sight of all those baked goods made it nearly impossible for me to not wolf down every single cookie as quickly as I could get my hands on them. In her frustration, Mom would eventually hit me with a spatula and call me things like "lard-ass," or "bucket-butt," or "a worthless little fat slob." And sure, those words were hurtful, but I didn't mind. Because I knew that I could salve my wounds with big fistfuls of sugar that were lovingly baked by a mom who was stuck with me. And I knew deep down that she loved me. She didn't have to say the words. Because once a year, she said it with cookies. That's what those Christmas cookies did for me. They filled me up, and comforted me, and were absolutely worth the searing heartburn and explosive diarrhea that usually crippled me each year at the end of every Christmas Cookie Day.

# Hanging Up My Stocking: "Oh Yeah! The Stocking!"

**So far** I have not lied to you, and at this point I don't see any reason to start. So let me tell you straight up that when I was a kid, I had no idea what the whole "hanging up your stocking" thing was all about. It never made any sense to me at all, but I always figured that if I ever said that, then Santa would label me "naughty" and pass me by. So I never even allowed myself to think about what a stupid custom it was until I was about twenty-eight years old, and even then, I wrote it on a piece of paper and showed it to my friend Cleveland before crumpling it up and throwing it out so that Santa's helpers didn't catch a whiff of it. Cleveland told me that the whole stocking thing started years ago—and I'm guessing it was way back in the Christmases before Christ. And the idea of it was that you would hang your stocking at the fireplace, and then Santa Claus would come down and fill it with toys. And if you weren't good, then Santa would put a lump of coal in your stocking, which would really suck, unless you were Superman, because then you could squeeze the coal really hard

*Naughty*

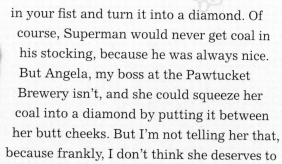

*Not Nice*

in your fist and turn it into a diamond. Of course, Superman would never get coal in his stocking, because he was always nice. But Angela, my boss at the Pawtucket Brewery isn't, and she could squeeze her coal into a diamond by putting it between her butt cheeks. But I'm not telling her that, because frankly, I don't think she deserves to know. But mostly Santa Claus fills the stockings with toys, which always leads me to this question—what kid in any time would want any toy that is small enough to fit inside a stocking? Huh? Riddle me that? You gonna find a Big Wheel inside a stocking? Or an Easy-Bake Oven? Come on! Even Rosie O'Donnell's corn-fed, adopted children probably don't have feet big enough to wear a sock you could fit a table-hockey game into. Everybody knows that the good stuff is always under the tree, and that, I believe, is how Jesus intended it. And if you think *that's* bad, isn't it a pain in the ass to hang a stocking from a brick fire-place? Ever try to push a thumbtack into a brick? You, my friend, may as well try and catch the wind. And sure, there's always duct tape, which will hold the stocking up, but it really looks like hell and also has that awful melting-plastic smell to it. Or, of course, some people who obviously have money to burn will go out and buy those decorative cast-iron stocking holders with the hooks on them that sit on the mantle and cost about twelve or fifteen dollars a piece. Can you believe that? What the hell could those people possibly need for Christmas? I don't know, but you can bet your sweet ass it wouldn't fit in a stocking. With all of this in

mind, you would think that the Christmas stocking is an obsolete relic, sadly past its prime, and no longer useful—like the butter churn or Andy Rooney. But you'd be mistaken, Buck Rogers, because Christmas stockings are still good for one thing and they serve a very valuable purpose, which I will now share with you. Every Christmas morning, after I had torn into all the wrapped packages under the tree—whether they were mine or not—I would at some point catch my breath and realize that as far as opening gifts, the fun was already over for another year. A sad wave of disappointment would start to wash over me. And then, I would remember that I still had stuff waiting for me in my stocking. It's like when you eat an entire thick-crust Caserta's Pizza from Federal Hill, and it's gone, and even though you couldn't eat another bite, you already miss the fun of eating that delicious pie. And then, just a few minutes later, you burp a really ripe, deep burp, and then—bam!—like magic, you're tasting pizza again! And that, if nothing, was the magic of my Christmas stocking. It was one more shot at gettin' stuff at the end of my Christmas morning, even if the stuff was stupid pencils with the Frito Bandito on them, or a Duncan Butterfly Yo-Yo, or a Ball in a Cup, or, even worse, a ripe apple and an orange, which my father would always point out were hard to find in the dead of winter, and were a very good source of fiber and nutrients, and which I, in spite of all of these facts, would annually pack into snowballs later in the day to throw at cars with my cousin Freddy.

# Christmas Vacation: "Two Weeks Out of School? Thank You, Jesus!"

**As if** all of the music and the food and the gifts weren't enough, my Christmas holiday also gave me an always too brief oasis of fun and freedom from the horror of going to school. It was awesome. I would wake up every morning and watch *The Price Is Right*—and this was back when Bob Barker still had black hair and cartilage in his knees and probably still had a wife who was alive, so he wasn't yet banging all those smokin' hot fashion models who show off all the great prizes and the cleavage of their great jugs on the show.

After that, I'd bundle up and join my friends for a fun day out in the snow. We would build a snowman and then I'd put a stick coming out of his crotch. And I'd say, "Ha! Look, that's his ding-dong!" And we'd all laugh. And then, my friend Head Hamel from down the street would put one of his mittens on the stick, and say, "Ha! Now he has a mitten on it!" And we would laugh some more. Oh, he was a schemer, that one. All day long with that kind of stuff. My mother hated him. One time, he took an extra snowsuit from his house and made a little snowman in it, and put it in an old plastic toboggan. He put a hat and gloves and a scarf on it, then pushed it down the hill and into the street in front of Lee's General Store. Some guy in a big Volvo tried to stop when he saw the toboggan come flying out into the road in front of him. But it was too late and he plowed right into it and the snowman got all mangled up under his car. The guy jumped out of his vehicle, all panicked-looking, because he thought he'd run over an actual kid. And that's when my friend Head Hamel ran down the hill, screaming, "You killed my brother!" Now, I've seen a lot of memorable things through the years at

Christmas, but I gotta tell you with all my heart that I have never seen anything like the look on that stupid driver's face. It was *priceless*!

And so were my many memories of Christmas vacations through the years, right up through high school, when I went to the James Woods Regional High's annual Winter Snow Ball with my all-time teenage heart-throb, Pheobe Diamond. Oh my God, I was so hot for Pheobe Diamond. She was everything that I wasn't—popular . . . a cheerleader . . . a girl. In September of my junior year, I vowed that I would ask her to the Winter Snow Ball, and by mid-December, about four days before the dance, I finally worked up the courage to try. I don't really remember what I said to her, because I was staring at her boobs, which were awesome, and I was yammering and babbling, like Betting Freddy on *The Flintstones*. But to my amazement, she said yes! It was the kind of moment that only happens to Corey Haim—in the movies I mean, because as I understand it, his life after child stardom was kind of a train wreck. But something magical was in the air for me, because at the time, I thought that Pheobe

Diamond saying she'd be my date to the Winter Snow Ball was nothing short of a Christmas miracle. I thought that right up until the evening of the dance, when I picked her up and she flatly told me that the only reason I was there was because she had been having a huge fight with her steady boyfriend, Joey Gambogi. Pheobe told me that guys like me were always asking her out all the time, and had been since the seventh grade when her wicked awesome boobs first popped out. As a result of their fight, she told Joey Gambogi that she would say yes to the first loser who was stupid enough to ask her to the Winter Snow Ball, just to piss him off. And as fate would have it, I had picked that exact moment to come stammering up to her at her locker, all trembling, with big, sopping pit stains under the arms of my Allman Brothers T-shirt. Now, you would think that's a crappy story, and for the most part it is, since she barely looked at me on the ride to the dance and once we got there, she spent the night either off in the corner having an animated fight with Joey Gambogi or smoking pot with the other popular girls in the ladies' room. Truth be told, as hot as she was, I wanted to kill her with my bare hands. But during the short ride home, that Christmas magic took over. As if setting the tone for a romantic winter's tale, the car radio suddenly played "Merry Christmas Darling" by the Carpenters. And if anything could thaw an icy moment, it was the rich and beautiful voice of Karen Carpenter, who was as lovely as she sounded, until she destroyed herself with a vicious cycle of binging and purging that escalated until she eventually starved herself to the point where she was so frail and boney that she snapped in two like a breadstick and died. My cousin Jimmy told me they buried her in one of those little suitcases like Paul Newman used to carry his two-piece custom-made pool cue in *The Hustler*. But of course, he's the same guy who told me Cindy Brady died when her maxi-coat got caught in the door of a school bus, so there's a pretty good chance that's probably a big load of bull. But at any rate, I was thankful that the Carpenter's were with me that evening, and it seemed as though their sweet Christmas song was having an effect on Pheobe, because as we a pulled up to her fancy house near Barrington Country Club, she actually spoke to me for the first time in hours. It's true, she never really ever looked at me, but I'll never forget the sound of her voice as she shrugged and said, "Well . . . thanks, I guess." My heart was racing as I saw her shift her weight as if to exit my father's car. And as I fought to control my emotions, which vacillated between unconditional adoration and unbridled rage, I struggled to speak. And with a mixture of both hope and hatred, I blurted, "Aren't you even going to kiss me goodnight?" Pheobe paused, then rolled her eyes as she heaved an irritated, guttural sigh. Then, reluctantly, she turned and leaned in toward me. For a moment, I was awash in a sea of warmth as I felt her moist bottom lip briefly press against my mouth, which was hanging open in stunned, gaping bewilderment. In a flash, I saw, ever so briefly, all the brilliance and promise of every Christmas I had ever known.

All the joy a young man could possibly experience in a lifetime was somehow compressed into this brief moment as her lovely young flesh pressed against mine. And then, just as quickly, she was gone—tearing into her house faster than Florence Griffith Joyner at the Olympic trials and wiping a loose film of my spit off her chin with the back of her delicate wrist. When we got back to school, she would later instruct me to never speak, or even make eye contact with, her ever again. And you can call me a cock-eyed optimist, but I didn't care. Because Pheobe Diamond had already given me more than I could have ever hoped for on that cold December evening so very long ago. It was my first date. My first kiss. And my first premature ejaculation. What a night!

# Christmas Specials: The Foundation of All That I Know About Christmas

**This may** come as a surprise to you, but I absolutely love television. And how could I not? Television is truly the one thing in my life that has never lied to me, especially when I was a kid. Unlike my father, television was always there. And unlike my mother, it was always on, and not just when it was drunk or relieved that it wasn't pregnant after all. Each night, I would plant myself on the braided rug in front of my parents' television and be whisked away to a colorful world of hope and excitement and adventures. And at no time were those adventures more spectacular than during the weeks between Thanksgiving and Christmas, when the three networks would roll out all the classic holiday specials that still resonate with me today. And remember, this was before VCRs and DVDs, so you had *one* night a year to catch these shows. Now you can buy them for $3.99 at the freakin' car wash, but back then, no kid ever dared to be away from the TV during the Christmas season—especially me! Even McDonald's had special holiday commercials where happy carolers would sing, "Give a hamburger to someone you like. Give some fries and a shake, and make someone happeee! Give a cheeseburger and fries to your favorite gal or your favorite guy. It's fun to give, it's fun to get . . . a little bit of McDonald's!" This, of course, was a song about

McDonald's gift certificates, which were fifty cents each, or a book of ten for five dollars. Now, I'm no math scientist, but you can bet your sweet ass that there's some serious savings going on in that deal. But we're here to talk about my favorite Christmas specials and what they've taught me through the years. As we go through my list, I'm sure you have a few of your own that aren't mentioned here. Well, feel free to add them, but do it on your own time, okay, because I'm really not that interested.

## Rudolph, the Red-Nosed Reindeer

Based on the famous story of a plucky reindeer who overcomes a life-long battle with fetal alcohol syndrome to one day guide Santa's sleigh through fog, there is nothing about this fantastic television special that isn't absolutely awesome. The songs are great, the acting is superb, and the claymation figures move and talk like actual puppets—especially the folksy, banjo-playing, Burl Ives snowman, who I believe was played by a young Wilford Brimley. Most people remember the heroic journey of Rudolph, who went out into the woods, and grew antlers and a pair of nuts, and then went back to Christmas Town and told every one to go to hell, especially Olive, the other reindeer, who used to laugh and call him names. But the real story here—or the secret story, as some us like to call it—was about Hermey, the misfit elf who wanted to be a "dentist." Now, they couldn't say what that really meant when this show was made back in the 1920s, but I think we all know what he meant by "dentist," am I right? Think about what a dentist does—filling cavities . . . giving oral exams . . . dressing up as Judy Garland on Halloween and getting drunk on

Santa's workshop for years has adhered to a strict "Don't Ask, Don't Tell" policy.

vodka and crying about how he can't ever go home for Thanksgiving dinner because his father never accepted his "dentist"-ness. You with me? Yeah. He's a trouser pilot. Like Brian's cousin Jasper. But this story reminds us that everyone has something to offer, even if we think a lot of what they do in the privacy of their own home is disgusting and a crime against nature. And think about it, without people like Hermey, who would design our clothing or produce our awards shows or make truly great movies like *Show Girls*? And why, you ask, would those guys want to show Elizabeth Berkley and Gina Gershon getting it on in a movie, knowing full well it would only appeal to guys like you and me who are not dentists? Well, I'll tell you why. Because it's a gift. And though many of us only share this spirit at Christmastime, these guys, in spite of all that's been done to them, know that it is better to give than to receive. Although I have noticed that a lot of the more effeminate dentists would rather receive than give. Some of them are even called "power receivers," which really makes me clench up my button when I think of it. But honestly, it's the dentists who really like to *give* that scare the hell out of me. You know, those quarterbacks, or rough cowboys, or big tough scary Marine dentists. I'm terrified of those guys. Because you could go camping with one of 'em by mistake . . . and what if he does it to you in the tent while you're sleeping . . . and . . . well . . . what if you *like* it? I mean, we all get lonely, right? Everybody likes to feel wanted. I just wouldn't ever want to have to sort all those feelings out, and frankly, it petrifies me. But, what the hell, it's at Christmas that we learn to put those fears aside. So, Merry Christmas, dental community! And thank you for the Broadway musical. Except for *Rent*. That one really sucked eggs.

## A Charlie Brown Christmas

**H**ard to believe, but when I was a kid back in the sixties, the comic strip *Peanuts* was as big as anything in the entertainment world, including Elvis, the Beatles, and Moms Mabley, the Satchel Paige of elderly, toothless, black-women stand-up comics. But as popular as this classic TV special was and still is, it would never have been created in this day and age. I say this not because people in these modern times are too jaded to believe that simply wrapping Linus's blue security blanket around a pathetic sapling would transform it into a beautiful, full, and decorated Christmas tree, but because of the fact that in today's world, Charlie Brown, like most kids I know, would absolutely have been put on an expansive cocktail of mood-enhancing pharmaceuticals. My God, have you ever seen a more clinically depressed kid than Charlie Brown? Every time I watch that show, I scream, "Good lord, get that kid on something, before he decides to end it all and possibly take one of us with him!" And what's he doing hanging with that crowd anyway? Especially Lucy. What a horrible, ball-breaking bitch that chick was. Imagine the poor bastard who ended up with her? I kid you not, if I ever found myself married to that freakin' Lucy, I would have stuck a gun in my mouth and shot it, like William H. Macy in *Boogie Nights*. That stupid Lucy was a lousy friend,

and on top of that, a very bad psychiatrist. For example, early in the story, Charlie Brown shows up at her makeshift outdoor office seeking help with his holiday depression. Now, any shrink worth his or her salt would have immediately put him on Paxil or Ambien, but what does Lucy do? She puts him in charge of the big Christmas pageant, knowing full well that nobody was gonna give him any respect—not even his damn dog. The poor kid would have been better off if the whole Peanuts gang lined up to squat over his head and take a dump on him. Still, isn't that piano music great? So freakin' catchy. And the dancing is awesome, especially the one kid doing that funny "head-hanging" dance, and those two happy offset twins dancing like go-go girls on *Hullabaloo*. And there's also that kid Sherman doing a very funny "sleepwalking" dance. You MTV fans out there might recognize that dance as an early-sixties precursor to the Running Man, which was invented in the early nineties by MC Hammer, and which made him a household name until he blew all of his money on Slim Jims and big, baggy parachute pants and ended up having to take a job at the post office. But anyway, not to spoil the ending, Charlie Brown did not shoot himself. Instead he sucked it up and suffered internally, doing all he could to get through another holiday season alone and unloved. And that, in spite of whatever scripture Linus may quote under dramatic stage lighting, is what Christmas is *really* all about. So, Merry Christmas, Charlie Brown. And screw you, Lucy.

> If I were to receive a partridge in a pear tree, I would hope that it was Laurie Partridge. Although on a bad day, I wouldn't swat back Shirley Partridge either. And then I would just rub it in Reuben Kincaid's face, 'cause he really wanted to get with her.

# Frosty the Snowman

This holiday classic was made by the same bunch of guys who made *Rudolph*, but they must have run out of Play-Doh, because the whole thing is a cartoon instead of the much-cooler-looking clay

stuff. Or maybe they just left the tops off of their Play-Doh and it got all hard and worthless. I hate when that happens because it even loses that good Play-Doh smell, and when that happens, that Play-Doh is gone, baby. And you can pour as much water on it as you want, but it's never gonna get squishy again. It's just gonna be a big puddle of water on the floor—which is how Frosty ends up near the end of this thing, because he saves the little blond-haired girl from freezing her cute little cartoon ass off by bringing her into a greenhouse full of those red Christmas flowers.

I don't know—something about a mean magician wanting his hat back, and Santa Claus ends up having something to do with it, but he's really shoehorned in. All I remember, really, is that the little girl had the cutest nose, and when I was nine, I wished she was in my class so I could stare at her all day and sit near her on the bus. She kind of looked like what I'm guessing Meg Ryan probably looked like when she was little, and I'm sure you're thinking, "Okay, I'm with you now. I could get with that." Well, not so fast, buster, because your mind will get turned around just like mine did when you find out that the girl's voice came from June Foray. That's right, Rocky the flying squirrel from Rocky and Bullwinkle. Imagine that? A budding Meg Ryan on the outside, but inside, a plucky, adventurous, and possibly homosexual rodent. "You can't judge a book by its cover" is not a lesson usually associated with Christmas, but thanks to *Frosty the Snowman*, we've just learned something that will serve us all for a lifetime, and that I wish I had remembered last year when I offered a ride to that beautiful, deep-voiced Filipino "girl" outside the Drunken Clam.

## Santa Claus Is Coming to Town

The good news is that those same guys must have gone out and got some new Play-Doh to make this classic special, where a mailman played by Fred Astaire makes up a whole bunch of stuff to explain the story of Santa Claus. The bad news is that they didn't find enough, because even though the songs are great and there's a lot of funny crap in here—especially the Burgermeister Meisterburger—for some reason this thing doesn't look anywhere near as good as *Rudolph* did. Maybe they shot their wad with *Rudolph*, you know? Like Sylvester Stallone did with *Cobra*—for my money, still

his finest film. Of *course* he couldn't make a sequel to *Cobra*. There was simply no way to improve on the original. But there's plenty of room for improvement on this thing. For starters, Fred Astaire was widely known as the greatest dancer ever—until Savion Glover was whipped up in a lab using a sperm from Sammy Davis Jr. and an egg from Gregory Hines. But in *Santa Claus Is Coming to Town*, his dancing is lousy. He's all stiff and awkward and creaking around, like my auntie Phyllis after unsuccessful back surgery. And oh, sure, the birds and wood creatures are all singing and acting like he's still got it, but he's just embarrassing himself out there. Then later, Santa Claus's future wife, Jessica, is singing some boring song that has nothing to do with Christmas, and she ends it by looking at her own reflection in a fountain. But you don't have to look too close to see that it's just a cardboard picture of herself in the bottom of the water! Did those guys think we wouldn't pick up on that? As a kid, that scene drove me nuts every time I saw it. As a grown-up, it only makes me realize how freakishly fat Jessica got years later when she became Mrs. Santa Claus. And what a waste it was, because she was really smokin' hot. Sometimes I wonder if Santa Claus made her stay that fat, the same way that Lucille Ball did to Vivian Vance. And in this case, it wouldn't surprise me at all, because Santa in this story was played by the always delightfully loopy Mickey Rooney—a true showbusiness legend and the living inspiration for "Mickey Rooney's Crazy Pills." So it was probably easy for him to play a guy who was so crazy he would willingly want to destroy a beautiful woman's body with rolls of hideous, marbled pork suet. And if that wasn't bad enough, how about a guy so crazy he would sit in the center of town, pull kids onto his lap, and tell them they'll get a toy, but only if they give him a *kiss*! Is he nuts? Think of the lawsuits! Isn't that how Michael Jackson lost his house and his nose? No wonder the Burgermeister slapped his ass in the dungeon! But all of this craziness is forgiven, though, when Mickey sings "Put One Foot in Front of the Other," another great song that has absolutely nothing to do with Christmas—any more than that annoying little penguin who follows him around and tries to steal every scene like Roberto Benigni.

# The Night the Animals Talked

This Christmas Special aired when I was a kid, but you'll have to take my word for it because I swear to God, I'm the only guy I know who remembers it at all. It was a cartoon about all the animals in the manger where Jesus was born because there was no room at the Holiday Inn, which they couldn't have known when they started their Christmas vacation because they didn't have Orbitz back then. And even if they did, it wouldn't have mattered because it's a safe bet that Jesus' parents probably didn't have a laptop. And even if they did, then *that*

wouldn't have mattered because they would probably have had dial-up, and it would have taken them forever to find a room. Their vacation would have been over by then. That's how slow dial-up is. Anyway, this special was a lot like an episode of *Twilight Zone*, except it wasn't scary, like the one where the spaceship lands on that old hag's house and she chops up all the little spacemen and throws one of them in the fire. And then she hacks up their spaceship with an ax, and the camera moves down and you see that the spaceship is from Earth! Holy crap, that scared the hell out of me. But this one isn't like that. It's more just weird, like when the guy who played the Penguin on *Batman* breaks his glasses and cries. You know that one? What's *his* problem? You're the only guy left on Earth, douche bag. Just go break into the Pearl Vision Center and take all the glasses you want. One of 'em will work and then you can read all you want, you big baby. Anyway, Jesus is coming, and for some reason, all the animals in the barn figure out that they can talk. It really wigs them out at first, but then after they get used to it, they all start talking a lot, because, well, they could never talk before, so naturally, they have a lot of catching up to do. And somehow, after the kid is born, they figure out that he had something to do with them being able to talk, 'cause, he's Jesus, right? So . . . okay, Christmas miracle. Now, a lot of animals, when they figure out that they can talk, for the most part they keep it to themselves. Like Mr. Ed. He never talked to anyone but Wilbur. And though a lot of people think horses are stupid—or at least the ass part of a horse—Mr. Ed was not stupid. Because he knew that if he went around town talking to people, the government would right away send a bunch of scientists over to knock him out and carve up his brains like a turkey trying to figure out what was making him talk, and they'd never figure it out, and he'd be dead. But these animals were so fired up about Jesus being born that they said they were gonna run all over town and tell everybody that their savior was here. And here's the weird part—Jesus, as little as he was, must have caught wind of this, because as soon as the animals hit the streets to tell everybody the joyous news, something happened and they couldn't talk anymore. So they ended up looking like just a bunch of stupid barnyard animals running around in the street, all mooing and bleating and clucking, and making the kind of racket in the night that makes me get out of bed and scream at my neighbor's dogs when I hear it. And the saddest thing about it was the looks on their faces. It always freaked me out because they could talk for a little while and then they couldn't, which didn't seem fair, but Jesus must have had a reason. And it sure is amazing that he has the power to shut somebody up when he doesn't want them to do his talking for him. But why he hasn't done this to Pat Robertson I will never know. Still, deep down, I guess I'm glad that the farm animals stopped talking. Because, if they did talk, it would make it harder for me to kill them, fry them, and eat them. I'd still do it. It just wouldn't be as easy, you know?

## Bing Crosby Christmas Specials

Nothing felt more like Christmas to me than the lavish sets and fake happiness of Bing Crosby and his second family, who every year did a one-hour Christmas special full of songs, dancing, and guest stars, like the great Jackie Gleason, and the not-quite-as-great John Byner. One time they all rode in a big sled with Michael Landon and his hair. Another time he did a long musical number with young Melba Moore, to which all of America said, "Who?" But the thing I still can't get over was the time he sang "The Little Drummer Boy" with David Bowie, who, when I was twelve, was reported to have been a gay Martian who escaped from Area 51 and recorded millions of records while on the run as he kept in constant motion to elude the authorities. It was shocking to see that freak standing next to Bing Crosby, who had played a priest in just about all of his movies. Their voices were so perfect together, but even then

I wondered if anybody had ever told old Bing that he would be sharing the stage with a guy who frequently wore dresses and was rumored to have had a three-way with his wife and Mick Jagger. Now, many of you may know that "der Bingle" had a first family with a different wife, years before these specials aired. And maybe you don't know that he wasn't as nice to that first wife and kids as he was to the second bunch. In fact, one of his older sons, who I think went on to be the hilarious malaprop comic Norm Crosby, wrote a searing tell-all book about how Bing used to verbally abuse them and then beat all of them senseless with huge pillowcases full of sweet Valencia Minute Maid oranges.

I will not stand here and defend these actions, in spite of my love for the man who gave us "White Christmas." But I will say that these horrible actions are *nothing* compared to what Bing did to his youngest son on his annual Christmas specials. That poor little kid couldn't sing for beans, and he had no business being out there. Bing's wife clearly dug the attention, and his daughter was really cute, and even got hot as the years went on. I think she even posed for *Playboy*, right around the time she shot Larry Hagman in his Malibu castle during a drinking binge in the seventies. And the older son could sort of sing and play the guitar a little. But that youngest boy was a disaster. And worse than hearing his flat, clunky singing was seeing that tragic look of pain in his eyes every year, in glorious

> I wish Fred "Rerun" Berry would come back to life. He would make us laugh, teach us to "pop-lock," and we all would have a Very Berry Christmas.

color, just in time for the holidays. It was the same look that the Vietnamese sniper girl had at the end of *Full Metal Jacket*, when she stared up at Matthew Modine and begged, "Shoot me. Please, shoot me!" Well, if I'd had a big Vietnam gun, I would've thought about doing anything I could to help the poor little guy—for the good of both of us. But in my house, we did not have a big Vietnam gun. Hell, we didn't even have remote control. But thank God we had Bing Crosby every Christmas. Right up until he croaked when I was about fifteen.

## Bob Hope Christmas Specials

Another thing we watched every year when I was growing up was the Bob Hope Christmas special, which actually aired about a week after Christmas. Why? Because unlike the ten or twelve truly awful specials he'd do every year, Bob Hope would be overseas for his Christmas special, entertaining our troops for the holidays. Yes, Bob Hope was always there for the soldiers. His annual Christmas show played all the big wars—Vietnam, Korea, World War II, the Battle of Vicksburg, the Trojan War, and that one near the end of *Empire Strikes Back*, in a galaxy far, far away. He was never afraid to put himself in harm's way and he always brought a really hot chick with him, like Joey Heatherton, or Raquel Welch, or Brooke Sheilds, or the "It" girl, Clara Bow. And every year, he'd trot one out onto the stage in front of thousands of men in uniform and say, "I just wanna remind you fellahs what you're fighting for!" And the soldiers would all go nuts laughing, and it was mostly a nervous laugh, because what Bob said really wasn't that funny, but the guys just had to blow off some tension by laughing because they'd been sitting out in a foxhole with a bunch of other dudes for months, getting shot at with no women around, and what they really wanted to do was run up onto that stage and bite Farrah Fawcett's pants off. But instead, they just laughed. And back home, so did my mom and I. Mom would pull her smoldering

81

Kent cigarette from her mouth, point it at the TV, and say, "That man, is a great American." And I would nod in agreement, as it would take me years to find out that Bob Hope was born in England. So he wasn't quite the Yankee Doodle Dandy we thought he was. And anybody that ever had to work or do business with him will tell you he wasn't really so great. And come on, I'll be the first one to say it . . . he really wasn't funny.

## KISS Saves Santa

Brighter and more life affirming than any Christmas miracle I will ever witness was the appearance of my all-time favorite Christmas special, *KISS Saves Santa*. Made on a limited budget in 1977, this classic holiday cartoon combines the two things I love in the world more than almost anything, up to and including my wife and children—the holiday season and the greatest band of all time, KISS! The story is a simple one: A wicked Winter Witch—played by young Kristy McNichol in a performance that displayed the dramatic chops which would later lead to her regular role as a very believable Miami police woman on the popular television series *Empty Nest*—is angry that her wickedness in the wintertime is always drowned out by the happy sound of Christmas carols from the tiny village of Littleville, where the witch lives on a mountain overlooking the town, and is always messing up its tiny citizens by freezing the sidewalks, so they're always falling and breaking their asses on it and stuff like that. Oh, and the other thing is that when they're not listening to Christmas carols, they're listening to KISS music. You'll see

why that's important later. Anyway, the witch finally decides that if she stops Christmas, then maybe the folks of Littleville will shut the hell up for a change, so she kidnaps Santa Claus—to which the great Gene Simmons would memorably say, "That does *not* rock!"—and then she hides him in a nest full of pterodactyl eggs, high above the city. Well, the mayor of Littleville, Mayor Tye Knee Funkerton—played by Nipsey Russell, which was also a very brave stretch because the script did not allow him to fall back on his short, cleverly written poems as he did so often on *The Match Game*. But he didn't need them. And I think this guy was a very underrated actor because he really sounded small here even though in real life, I'm guessing he was kind of tall—anyway, the mayor usually could take care of things on his own, but when he heard that this time Santa had been kidnapped, and Christmas was on the line, he knew just who to call. Because remember before what I said about them loving KISS? Well, KISS loved them, too, and soon the KISS-copter is in the air, and Paul, Gene, Ace, and Peter are on their way to save Santa with a tidal wave of fire breathing, blood-spitting, smoking guitars, and pyrotechnics. The songs are raucous and memorable, and Ace's dialogue is mercifully kept to a minimum. Listen closely for a young Ricky Schroder, as the small Dutch boy who happily announces that KISS has arrived to save the day. He says, "Look! I see a star in the east!" And Nipsey says, "That is no star in the east! That's Paul Stanley's face!" And just then . . . you see the famous star on Paul Stanley's face. Right when he says that! I don't know how they got that to happen, but, you just gotta see it for yourself. So go down to your local video store and ask if they have a copy

of *KISS Saves Santa*. And if they don't, then demand that they order you one. And write letters and make phone calls to every video outlet you can find until you drive them crazy. Do not take no for an answer. You will thank me, as I thank KISS every year, for saving Santa.

# Mr. Magoo's Christmas Carol

Okay, we've already kind of covered this one, remember? It's just great, and it's the very story that has brought us this far on our trip back to Christmas Spirit—or as Bob Cratchit would sing with Mr. Magoo, "A Christmas Far More Glorious Than Grand." I'll tell you, for a Dick, that Charles Dickens sure wrote some good songs for this thing. The problem is, nowadays very few people get to enjoy them, because this great Christmas special hasn't been seen in years. They don't show it on TV anymore, since it was discovered that Mr. Magoo was in fact legally blind, and apparently it's politically incorrect to laugh and be entertained when an old sightless guy goes careening down a busy sidewalk in his antique jalopy or mistakes a brass door knocker for a Chinese waiter and starts yelling at it. So I guess a bunch of blind people were offended and complained, which really makes no sense to me because—think about it—none of them has ever actually seen it, although I'm sure they might have read about it in one of their bumpy newspapers. But either way, as a result, they don't show *Mr. Magoo's Christmas Carol* anymore, and personally, I think that's just bogus.

And it's no wonder people lose their holiday spirit when such treasured stories of the past are taken away from them. That's why I never let this happen. I carry the messages of these great TV shows and the memories of all the Christmases of my past with me through the whole year, the same way that Daryl Hall carried John Oates through the better part of their two-decade-long reign of terror. And that, my friends, is why every year, I always have a ridiculously whompin' good time during the next part of our journey.

Part
Three

Christmas
Present

# Okay,

so picture this: It's halfway through Mr. Magoo's haunted Christmas Eve, and the Ghost of Christmas Past has just dropped him back off in his bed. And he's thinking maybe the whole thing was a nightmare, because he ate a whole bag of Doritos before he went to sleep . . . you know? And then he washed 'em down with a quart of Crystal Pepsi or something. It happens, 'cause I did that once, and I had this really messed up dream where the Dancing Bear from *Captain Kangaroo* came into my room with a handgun and he was really pissed off because I had taken him for a big pile of money in a card game. And when he went to shoot me I tried to put my arms up, but they weren't my arms—they were big oversized Jimmy Dean Pure Pork Sausages. And I woke up screaming and gnawing on my arms until they started bleeding, even though it was all just a dream. Now, I'm not totally blaming this awful dream on the Doritos or the Crystal Pepsi, so please, all you lawyers from the Frito-Lay company just get back in your big leather chairs and take a pill, because I'm not going to sue. However, you might want to consider putting a small warning label on your fine products that says, "Warning: When taken together before bed, these things may cause you to dream about a big gun-toting puppet bear, and you'll be so scared that you bite into yourself, hoping for breakfast meats." A label like that would have made me think twice about my late-night snackin'. But it wouldn't have done anything for poor old Mr. Magoo on that memorable Christmas Eve. Because just when he had convinced himself that he was dreaming about the Ghost of Christmas Past, Mr. Howell looked down at the end of his bed and saw a *second* ghost—the Ghost of Christmas Present!

Now, when I was a kid I always was a little confused because I thought he was saying he was the Ghost of Christmas "Presents." But this ghost didn't have any presents for Mr. Magoo, even though he was pretty fat and jolly, and frankly looked like he could have afforded to bring the old guy something, like a nice sweater at least. Which he really could have used, too, because before anyone could say, "That's enough, John Mayer," the Ghost of Christmas Present had already dragged Mr. Magoo back out into the freezing snow to give him a whirlwind, behind-the-scenes tour of his hometown during the Christmas season. And that's what I would

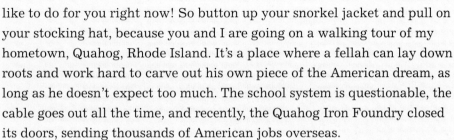

like to do for you right now! So button up your snorkel jacket and pull on your stocking hat, because you and I are going on a walking tour of my hometown, Quahog, Rhode Island. It's a place where a fellah can lay down roots and work hard to carve out his own piece of the American dream, as long as he doesn't expect too much. The school system is questionable, the cable goes out all the time, and recently, the Quahog Iron Foundry closed its doors, sending thousands of American jobs overseas.

But none of this matters to us at Christmas, when the streets of Quahog are festooned with strings of colorful lights, the storefronts are decked out with holiday greetings, and everywhere you look there are wreaths, bearing pine cones and holly berries—which, by the way, were named after actress Halle Berry, whose beauty is surpassed not even by all of the glorious sights of Christmas combined, *and* who showed us her sweet boobs in the movie *Swordfish*. It was an image that haunted me for quite some time, not only because she is as lovely a woman as I will ever see, but because when she opened that shirt and whipped out those prize-winning show dogs of hers, I hit "freeze frame" on the TiVo and practically went into a coma as I stared at them wide-eyed for hours. The next morning I realized I had passed out with the picture still frozen, and you can't do that because if you freeze-frame a picture too long on a TV it burns into the screen and stays there. So from then on, everything we watched in our home had a permanent gray-blue image of Halle Berry's naked jugs floating over it, which was nothing short of fantastic. Before then, I didn't think anything could possibly make television viewing even better for me, but needless to say, I was glued to the screen night and day. Of course, Lois pretty much figured out something was up when she saw that I was actually watching C-SPAN for hours on end, and before long we had to get a new TV. But, listen, before you put this book down and run out to rent *Swordfish*, let me show you around Quahog. We'll start in

the center of town at the giant Christmas tree and visit the homes of some
of my friends and neighbors to see how they are preparing for the holiday
season.

And if we're lucky, the Heat Miser will take that humbug out of his
butt just long enough to "Let It Snow," and soon my little town will be
covered in a beautiful, shimmering blanket of white. We can make snow
angels and catch flakes on our tongues and quietly stress out that we still

haven't put our snow tires on even though our wives have been screaming at us to do it since Veteran's Day, and now it's snowing, so she was right again, and I'm never going to hear the end of it. So come on. Let's get going before a warm Atlantic rain follows our Christmas snow, as it usually does, and the sun comes out, turning our Quahog Winter Wonderland into a filthy, depressing morass of brown slop. Besides, I need a beer, so let's start at my friend Cleveland's house.

# Christmas with Cleveland

**H**ey, everybody! And a very Merry Christmas to y'all. I'm taking a little holiday time off from the deli and was about to put on some Christmas carols, or maybe *James Brown's Funky Christmas*, while I decorate the tree and get the house all ready for Santa's big arrival. I've got a manger scene, a happy lighted Santa, and a big plastic snow globe for the lawn that I bought at the Quahog Pharmacy last year. But it seems to have a hole in it, because I'm having a whale of a time trying to get it inflated this year. You seem like you're surprised at my decorations. What—just 'cause I'm black, you expected to see all Kwanzaa decorations in here? I wouldn't know how to begin to decorate for Kwanzaa. As a Christian man, I celebrate Christmas. I honestly don't even know what Kwanzaa is. But I do know there are seven principles of Kwanzaa, which are listed on a pamphlet I received down at the Quahog African American League. I must admit that as I read the pamphlet, I was worried that they were gonna try to sell me something at the end. And I was saying to myself, "Look, I don't like what the white man has done to us either, but is all this necessary?" But, it turns out, there was no price attached to the spirit of Kwanzaa, and I realized that I do share its principles and values, which are as follows:

**UNITY.** Of course! We all need to get along.

**SELF-DETERMINATION.** Ain't nobody gonna tell me who I am, what I am, or how loudly I can talk back to the screen at a movie theater—ever again!

**COLLECTIVE WORK AND RESPONSIBILITY.** That's just brothers helping brothers, and we are *all* brothers. Well, except for Tyler Perry. Sometimes in his films he's more of a sister. But that's his right, so you go, girl!

**COOPERATIVE ECONOMICS.** My closets are packed with many fine garments that are made for us and by us. And for years I was one of the two or three dozen viewers who proudly and faithfully watched the now defunct UPN.

**PURPOSE.** I believe I was put here on Earth to be a loving husband, a dedicated father, and to provide hearty, delicious sandwiches with a wide array of sides to hungry Quahogians at affordable prices.

**CREATIVITY.** I just finished macraméing a complete set of place mats for my dining room table. Some people find macramé very tiresome, and a bit homosexual. But it relaxes me.

**FAITH.** There's no question where I stand on this principle. My faith in the lord, who was born on Christmas Day, dictates the way in which I choose to live my life—with a spirit of peace, love, and forgiveness. It is also a source of great racial pride for me, because anyone who actually takes the time to read the Bible rather than just preaching it will find more than enough evidence to support the true fact that Jesus was a black man. Just like Santa Claus and Babe Ruth. And Bill Clinton. Chew on that, honkies! Ah, I'm just playin'. Merry Christmas, everybody!

# Christmas with Quagmire

Hey there, gang! Welcome to my swingin' bachelor pad. I've already got the place all set to have a Cool Yule, and a truly Rockin' New Year's Eve. The mistletoe is hung above the door and my penis and I've got *A Dave Brubeck Christmas* on the hi-fi and a big bowl of eggnog, made with the perfect blend of Jamaican rum, Spanish fly, and roofies. Oh! Or, I guess what I should be saying is "Ho! Ho! Ho!," not only because that's what Santa says when he laughs, but because I have three

whores waiting for me in the next room! I've actually got five more on their way over. Later on, we're all gonna act out a scene from my favorite holiday video, which is called, *Eight Maids a-Milking*. Giggity-giggity-giggity! But don't worry, I'll let them wait, now that you're here. Friends are important—especially at Christmas. Now, this is the time of year when we all have to decide if we've been naughty or nice. And if you've been naughty—and you're a chick—I want you to come on inside and make yourself comfortable. And if you've been nice—or you're a dude—why don't you go next door and see Cleveland? He loves company, and I think he needs help blowing up that stupid snow globe that everybody wasted a hundred bucks on last year. Go on. Get out of here, okay, guys? I mean it. Happy Christmas. Go blow up that snow globe.

Meanwhile, ladies, I might need you to blow on something over here, but it won't be a snow globe! Oh! Aw-right! Oh course, by that I mean that we're all gonna blow out the candles later, after we sing "Happy Birthday" to the baby Jesus. It's a ritual I maintain every year out of respect for the glory and the wonder of this holy season. And when that's done, I will say a solemn prayer, thanking the lord for all of his blessings at Christmas. And *then*, I am gonna bend each one of you broads over my knee and spank your bare bottoms for being naughty! Oh! And that's when Jolly Old St. Glenn will *really* get down to business. You better believe there won't be any "Silent Night" around here when I get going, and there won't be a dry seat in the house. I am gonna trim your tree, fill your stockings, come down your chimney, unwrap your package, empty my sack, and jingle your bells. Aw-right! And then maybe, if you're up to it, we'll have sex. Whatever you want. It's up to you, naughty girls. You into pain? I got a whip in my den. We could put

that "Sleigh Ride" record on and I could crack your ass on cue with the whip sounds. That's always fun. Or you could whip me, if that floats your boat, because if anyone's been naughty this year, it's me, you're old buddy Quagmire. Now, I can't promise that I will want you here when I wake up in the morning. And I can't promise that I'll even want to know, let alone remember, your name. But I will promise you that even though Christmas only comes once a year, this will not be the case with you. Because I was raised to believe that Christmas is a season for giving. And in the spirit of that belief, I am gonna give it to you all night long. I'll give and give and give until you're a quivering mass, huddled up in a ball on my shag carpet, crying tears of both pleasure and pain, and softly blowing puffs of air onto the fresh rug burns on your knees and elbows. And you know what the best part of all of this is? Santa will be watching. He's always watching, that kinky bastard. And that's okay, too. Because that's my way of giving something back to him. So Merry Christmas, Santa. And you're welcome, ya big, fat, peeping freak! Giggity-giggity-giggity! Aw-right.

## Christmas with Joe

Well, hello there, neighbors, and season's greetings to all of you. You can come on in, although Bonnie has gone to bed. She's a little tuckered out from wrapping gifts, and decorating, and once again baking this fantastic gingerbread house as she does every year at Christmas. She also got a little rattled a few moments ago because I took out my service revolver and shook it in the air and went into a screaming jag about how I wanted to kill somebody. I have to say it's a little disappointing to me, because she's known me long enough to understand that I didn't mean her. But still, she ran from the room, sobbing, and once again threatening to move back in with her folks if I keep

this up. I guess there's no reasoning with a woman once her "pregnancy hormones" kick in, but you seem like logical folks, so let me assure you that you are not in any danger, even though my gun is still loaded and lying there on the table next to the gingerbread house, and even though that half-empty bottle of Jack Daniel's would tell even the most amateur detective that I am every bit as cocked as that pistol.

Now, I know that this is supposed to be a joyous time of the year, and I promise you that I do what I can to make the most of it. But Christmas is also a very difficult season for me, because it marks the anniversary of what was perhaps the worst thing I've ever had to endure.

It happened on a Christmas, years ago, when I was a patrolman over on the east side of Providence. It's a fine, upscale neighborhood, with many colonial homes of historical significance, and I was almost done with my shift that evening when I saw something suspicious. Now, I am not, nor have I ever been a racist cop, but when I saw a green, furry man running around the affluent east side with a large sack slung over his shoulders, it was obvious to me that this gentleman was in the wrong neighborhood and was up to no good. As sharp as my eye was that evening, my preoccupation with the Christmas holiday season impaired my judgment, because I should have called for backup. This was no ordinary perp. It was the Grinch. I'd heard about him. I'd read his rap sheet and his warrants many, many times. He was dangerous. A real scumbag with shoes too tight and a heart three sizes too small. And he fought with the strength of ten Grinches, which I found out only after confronting him on the roof of the Providence Orphanage. A struggle ensued, and moments later I was lying on the ground, my eyes fixed on the stars in the cold, clear nighttime sky. And as I lay there in the freshly fallen Christmas snow, I said three things to myself. The first thing was "I should have called for backup." The second was "Dammit! I still have a ton of gift-wrapping to do back home." And the third was, "OH MY GOD, I'M PARALYZED!! I CAN'T MOVE MY LEGS!! SWEET JESUS, PLEASE HELP ME MOVE MY LEGS!! NO-O-O-O-O-O-OO!!"

You know, Elvis Presley once sang about a blue Christmas, and everybody felt bad for him. But I don't think Elvis ever knew what it was like to spend Christmas sitting in the dark, with lifeless legs and a large Ziploc bag of his own urine taped next to him. And yet, when I think of all that I have at Christmas, with hearth and home and family and friends, I realize that it's wrong for

me to sit here moping and cursing and hollowing out the tips of bullets, filling them with liquid arsenic, and then sealing them over with wax. Maybe you should take this gun, by the way. And be really careful with it, because I'm really wasted, so I'm sure I spilled arsenic everywhere. But it's time to sober up. It's Christmas, and I need to keep looking forward. Hell, we have a baby on the way! And if it's a boy, he'll need his dad to nurture him, and teach him, and help him grow up big and strong, just like my other son—who I haven't seen in a while. In fact . . . I don't think anyone has seen him in a while. Oh my God. My son is missing! Where the hell did he go? I can't imagine it's possible that I had anything to do with it. Or did I? You know what . . . you should really take that gun away from me. It'll be my gift to you. Merry Christmas to you, now. I really have to go talk to Bonnie.

This may be the eggnog talking, but when Johnny Mathis sings his rendition of "Sleigh Ride," I swear to God I can feel some of my toes tapping.

# Christmas With Herbert

**W**ell, hello there, children! I see you all out there playing in the snow and getting your little snow pants all wet. You know the weather outside is frightful. So you want to come into my house and dry yourselves off by the fire? I could get you out of those wet clothes and rub your little rosy-red cheeks to get you all warmed up. No? How about some hot cocoa, then? I make it with real milk, which is good for growing youngsters. Rogers Hornsby used to drink a big glass of cold milk before every game. I saw him play once when he came to the Polo Grounds. That man could really swing the old hickory. And he had big, strong, ripply arms like a longshoreman. Mmmm. Come on inside, and I'll tell you all about fighting the Germans in World War I. I won't bite you. I can't bite you, because I don't have any teeth. Neither does my dog, Jessie. He's asleep under the Christmas tree right now. You'll like that, because it's one of those new-fangled, white aluminum trees with red and silver balls, and a modern color wheel that changes the white tree from red to blue to green to yellow as it turns. But it hasn't worked for a few Christmases because it needs a new bulb and I can't get anyone to go to the store for me. Hey, look what

103

I have around the tree! It's a train set. Just like the *Polar Express!* You like that book? I sure do. All those children riding on that train in their PJ's, all the way to the great big North Pole. Mmmmm. Come take a look at this train! You can follow it all around the tree, and in and out of a tunnel . . . and then, where's it going?

Why it's going all the way down to the basement! You should follow it, I'll bet there's a whole bunch of candy canes down there! No? Well, all right. I guess we have time. Easter Sunday's coming. And the Easter Bunny's gonna fill my whole house with marshmallow Peeps and chocolate eggs for you to hunt. You won't want to miss that! Until then, just don't forget that for all the joyful people you'll meet this Christmas, there are just as many lonely people in the world. And you just might be able to brighten their day by giving them a wave, or sending a card, or gettin' your fat ass down those stairs. Okay, I guess I'd better go check and see if Jessie's still breathing. I sure hope he isn't dead! Merry Christmas!

## Christmas with Mort Goldman

Hello, and come on in, but please use the mat to wipe your feet. It's not that I think you have germs, but sometimes in winter there are all sorts of horrible things lurking under the snow, like a spilled milk shake or fecal matter from a cat and the next thing you know it's all over the carpet in our living room, which we just had steamed for the holidays. I like to keep my house in order, which is a custom of my people, and in a way relates to the holiday we were in the middle of celebrating when you arrived, which you may have noticed by now is not Christmas but Hanukkah.

Oh my goodness. With all those geese a-laying, swans a-swimming, calling birds, french hens, turtle doves, and partridges, is it any wonder that we're living with the constant threat of a bird flu pandemic?

Hanukkah celebrates the rededication of the Holy Temple in Jerusalem by our people, who were led by Judah Maccabee and his soldiers, after some Greeks and hooligans broke into the temple and had themselves a regular shindig. When Judah and his army arrived, the place was just a mess. The hooligans had broken everything—including the golden menorah, which is just a sin. But God was once again on our side—and anyone who doesn't think so should take a ride by the temple here in Quahog on any given Saturday and check out the fine array of luxury cars in the parking lot. Not a clunker in the bunch! And anyway, when Judah lit the menorah, it miraculously burned for eight days, which gave them enough light to clean up the great big mess left by the Greeks and hooligans.

Yes, I know you probably don't think that's a very good story. It's certainly not as sexy and cinematic as a deer with a red lightbulb on his nose or a virgin birth in a manger, but it's a story that has always resonated with our people, including my son, Neil. He's a regular book worm, my Neil. And after reading up on the history of Hanukkah, he suggested to me that the hooligans in question were simply free-thinking Jews who wanted to embrace and accept other philosophies that were emerging from the Dark Ages as the planet evolved. Neil suggested that the seizing of the temple was an affront to the evolution of civilization, or at the very least an effort to squelch freedom of thought. I found this to be very progressive thinking from that little man of mine. And Muriel and I don't like that around here, so I had to hit him very hard with my slipper. He's fine now, though. He's in his room, quietly spinning his new dreidel. Oh, he can spin it like a champ, my Neil. And he'll be in there spinning it alone and making atonement for his views while outside, all the Christian kids are running amok and just going absolutely bonkers. The custom of the dreidel probably doesn't make sense to you either, but that's fine. It's always been my belief that we can all live together in peace, despite our differences. Just as long as you remember that if you ever even think about putting up a Christmas tree, or a bell, or a snowman decoration in an airport without including a menorah, you better believe that I will be there to make a great big stink about it as fast as my legs can carry me. Happy Holidays, everybody! Would you like a potato latke? No, I know. No one ever does.

## Christmas with Mayor West

Hello, fellow citizens! And may the season's bright blessings be with all of you! I simply love this time of year, when I can finally put on my festive Victorian garb and stroll through the center of town offering happy tidings, without drawing anywhere near the same amount of questionable stares and scornful looks that I get when I wear my festive Victorian garb to the beach in the summertime. But I wear your scorn as a badge of honor, all you sad folks who have forgotten how exhilarating it can be to stroll down the avenue in full, turn-of-the-

If something isn't done about global warming, Santa's workshop may soon be under twelve feet of water. Go green, everyone!

century formal regalia—or as it's known in certain musical circles—"gay apparel"! And to all my gay constituents, "Happy Gay Christmas, too!" I acknowledge and try to pay homage to the holiday customs of all the good men and women of this fair city, even the ancient festival of Tet, which will be celebrated later in the month by Quahog's small yet thriving Vietnamese community, as dictated by the reliable lunisolar calendar of the ancient Chinese. I'm aware that this rankles the hides of many of the Vietnam War vets in town, who, for understandable reasons, still find the very word "Tet" offensive. But I don't take my cue from them. Nay, I say to you that my actions are dictated by one man, and one man alone. And that man is Good King Wenceslas, Duke of Bohemia, who in the dead of winter of the year 936, told his staffers to walk in his footsteps through the snow, wherein they found that heat was in the very sod in which the sainted king had printed! By following his every step, they found that their feet were never affected by the cold. Can you imagine this? He had magical, heat-generating feet! And this was over a thousand years ago in Prague! Boy, if I could pull that off, not only would it boost the spirits of cold-footed people everywhere, but I could make a fortune! Or at least be featured on David Letterman's "Stupid Human Tricks." So follow me, if you'd like. And perhaps you'd like to carry my caged wren for me. As is the custom in Ireland, a wren is carried door to door on the feast of St. Stephen. At every door, we will cajole the occupant to give us something for the wren to eat, like a big lump of pudding or a warm bowl of mutton broth. Of course, it's understood that the provisions we gather will not be for the bird at all. It's all a clever ruse, you see? And if we hit the streets at the right hour, we will all eat like *kings*—better even than Good King Wenceslas himself. And he was a king who was known for some good eating. But if not, it's no matter, because at the very least, we can always eat the wren. And I don't know if it's the holiday season that's gotten a hold of me, but I have got a hankering for a tasty mouthful of raw, panicked, wing-flapping wren. Mmm! That tasty little fellah may not even make it to the town square! Happy Christmas, everybody! And "Cung chuc tan xuan, An hang thinh vuong" to you all!

# Christmas Through the Eyes of My Family

**Well,** we're back on Spooner Street, outside the home of the people I'm stuck with every Christmas—my family. You know what they say: "You can pick your friends, and you can pick your nose, but you can't tune a fish." No, wait . . . "You can't pick a piano . . ." Hold on. Ah, screw it. Welcome to the Griffin home, the smart but modest dwelling that I once turned into a giant puppet for my own bemusement. It's a lot like the Waltons' home at Christmastime—all full of cheer, and spirit, and possibly in-bred children with odd-shaped heads and ill-fitting clothing. Maybe later, Cleavon Little will stop by and we'll all ride an old-fashioned sleigh over to the Baldwin ladies' home for a sampling of their

I have some gifts for you. They're up in my bum!

"Papa's Recipe"—which everybody on Walton's Mountain knew was moonshine whiskey. That would really be something, because he was so damn funny in *Blazing Saddles*, and the combination of him and homemade hard liquor would have guaranteed that we'd all be laughing all the way on *that* sleigh ride. But, it isn't going to happen, because, sadly, he's been dead for years. So instead, come on in and meet my family!

## Christmas Thoughts from Chris

Ha-ha! Hi, everyone! Merry Christmas! I'm so excited and hopped up on sugar that I almost can't even stand it! There's no school this week. And it's snowing! I'm gonna get in a snowball fight and go sliding. And I really want to take a big slushy mitten full of wet snow and drop it down the front of Meg's shirt, so she'll scream. And then when the cold water hits her small boobies, her nipples will pop out like that little thermometer on our Christmas turkey. And I can point and laugh at her and yell, "Neeples! Neeeeeee-heeeee-heee-ples!" Ha-ha. But really, I won't do that, at least not until after Christmas, because Santa Claus is coming! And I think I've been pretty good so far this year, so I don't want to spoil it for myself right when I'm coming down the home stretch to getting a whole bunch of cool stuff for Christmas. He's coming! I'm so excited, I can't wait! Can you believe that dude packs up a whole sled full of toys and makes his way to every house in the world in one night? Man, that's quite a job for a really old fat guy whose cholesterol levels are probably hovering dangerously in the high three hundreds. One of these days he's going to pop a vein and drop dead if he's not careful. I sure hope it's not in my lifetime—especially this year, because I've got quite a list of stuff I want him to bring. Boy it's gonna be hard to go to sleep on Christmas Eve. Of course, it's hard for me to go to sleep on any evening, because there's an Evil Monkey who lives in my closet. Why he's there I will never know and what he's got against me is an even bigger mystery. And what's with the evil vibe all the time? I've never been able to figure that out. But last week I was watching *Home Alone*, and Macaulay Culkin was talking to that scary old neighbor of his, who he thought was a psycho killer, but it turned out he was just sad because his daughter hated him. And Macaulay Culkin told the scary dude to call his daughter, or whatever, and it worked because she came to visit and the scary guy cried, and it was a happy ending—unless the guy really *was* a psycho killer and then he killed his daughter, which we'll never know because the cameras didn't follow them into his house. But anyway, that gave me the idea that maybe I could change the Evil Monkey by doing something nice for him, and I decided that even though he's always scaring the hell out of me, I would buy him a Christmas present. So the other day I went down to Warwick Shopper's World and tried to pick out some-

Last Christmas I fell backward into a snow drift, and boy, didn't *that* make my brown eye blue!

thing that I thought a monkey would love. I chose a banana, and Gwen Stefani's *Love. Angel. Music. Baby.* CD, both of which were readily available at Warwick Shopper's World, which has always been known for its selection and competitive prices. I wrapped the gifts in a box and left it outside the slightly open door of my closet. And that night, as I was trying to go to sleep, the door creaked open wide. The Evil Monkey was about to point at me in his menacing way when he noticed the small package at his feet. He opened it and looked inside, and for a moment, I saw his Evil Monkey face soften. The harsh lines on his furrowed brow seemed to disappear, and his eyes, that for so long had frightened me with their fiery venom and unmasked hatred, suddenly seemed soft and sad to me. In a moment that seemed an eternity, we stared at each other—a gentle truce in what had thus far been a very adversarial relationship. I took the opportunity to give him a warm and caring smile. And I could see that in his heart, he wanted to do the same. But instead, he quickly did a doody in his hand and flung it at me before returning to the closet, slamming the door behind him. I know it was probably unrealistic to think I could have changed him in one moment. But at least I know I did a good thing. Probably good enough to balance out throwing slush down Meg's shirt, which, man, oh, man, I can't wait anymore—I just have to do it! See you later, Wally Gators! Ha-ha! Mom! I'm going outside!

## Christmas Thoughts from Meg

Hi everyone, it's me, Meg Griffin. One time when I was eight, I watched a Christmas episode of *Reading Rainbow* and LeVar Burton had a book called *The Little Match Girl* by Hans Christian Andersen. It was a sad story about a girl who sells matches in the dead of winter, and she can't go home without selling any matches,

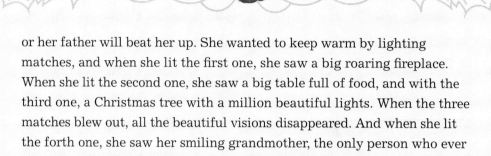

or her father will beat her up. She wanted to keep warm by lighting matches, and when she lit the first one, she saw a big roaring fireplace. When she lit the second one, she saw a big table full of food, and with the third one, a Christmas tree with a million beautiful lights. When the three matches blew out, all the beautiful visions disappeared. And when she lit the forth one, she saw her smiling grandmother, the only person who ever loved her. The grandmother took her up in her arms and flew away. And the next morning, they found the Little Match Girl lying dead in the snow.

For years after that, I would stand at the window in my room and light wooden matches as I looked out into the winter's night. But I didn't want to see visions of fireplaces, or food, or Christmas trees. I wanted to see me, outside, lying dead in the snow. Or at least some-place where people listened to me and didn't take every chance they could to call me stupid, or fat, or the result of a broken condom. Of course, the matches never worked. One time when I lit one, my father walked by my bedroom door. He rushed in and I thought he was going to scold me for play-ing with matches. But, instead, he just took the match from me, held it to his butt, and lit a fart with it. He laughed like a hyena, and as depressed as I was, I have to admit, it really was something to see that blue/green flame shoot out of him ever so briefly. At that point, it was as close to a bonding moment as I'd ever had with my father. And it gave me hope that someday, there would be better Christmastimes for me. At least better than the Christmas when I was thirteen and my mother felt compelled to put a can of feminine hygiene

spray in my stocking, and then told me what it was for, right in front of my brother Chris. Later on, during our holiday dinner, Chris and my father couldn't wait to tell my entire extended family that I was "not so fresh down there."

One year at Christmas, I had just seen *The Sisterhood of the Traveling Pants*. I wanted to pretend I was the fifth sister of their sisterhood, and I would put on jeans and write down all of my innermost thoughts in a diary to share with the other girls, especially Amber Tamblyn, who seemed nicer than the rest of them. So I asked for a diary for Christmas. A special one, with a leather cover, and maybe one of those little padlocks and keys so no one would read it. What I got that Christmas morning was a spiral-bound notebook with a picture of Moesha on it. And this was years after her show was off the air. I swear to God, my mother must've gotten it from the ninety-nine cent store. I wanted to throw it out, but then I would've felt bad for Moesha. She didn't do anything wrong. And besides, Christmas for me is all about making the best of what you've got. I believe in my heart that if I keep doing that, somehow my life will get better someday. It has to. It couldn't possibly get any worse than it has been. So I took my Moesha notebook upstairs and I sat on my bed and wrote myself a little Christmas poem. You're the first person I have ever shared it with, so if you don't mind, while you're reading, it would really mean a lot to me if you could pretend you're Amber Tamblyn. Okay, here's my poem . . . "sistahs."

### "Christmas" by Meg Griffin
*Hang your stocking Christmas Night,*
*Pray for Peace, and Love and Light.*
*And should you get a lump of coal,*
*Then burn it bright to warm your soul.*

Merry Christmas everyone. And thank you for listening. I love you, Amber Tamblyn. You're my best friend in the whole world. Oh, and by the way, *please* don't ever show this to my father. Or anyone.

## Christmas Thoughts from Stewie

Season's Greetings, good people! But, oh, please don't look at me, I am just a mess! I've been in here all day trying to get my Christmas cards done. It all really sneaks up on you, doesn't it? I told myself they'd be in the mail on the day after Thanksgiving this year, and then—whoops!—hello, I'm Mr.

Hey idiots! This Christmas let's all remember what Reagan taught us in the eighties—greed is good!

To: Kim Jong Il

Last-Minute-Hustle-and-Bustle again! I can see from your expression that you're rather surprised to see me caught up in the banal trappings of the holiday season, and I must admit, even I find it a bit disturbing to be a willful participant in rituals that as a rule I would generally find pedestrian at best. I really *do* have better things to do than address and mail out eighty-five greeting cards with a photo of me sitting on Santa's lap at the mall. It was a choice between that or myself with Brian, but I absolutely despise it when people send me pictures of their dog. ("Oh, he's wearing funny antlers, isn't that a stitch?") Mark my words, a day may come when those cretins will rue the inclusion of a return address on their insipid cor-

**ME WITH SANTA**

respondence. That notwithstanding, I must confess that in spite of myself, I've actually come to enjoy the holidays. And the truth is that I've got the rest of my life to take over the world, enslave its people, and rule with a merciless iron hand. But for now, I'm a baby, dammit, and it's Christmas! It's all so much fun! All the singing, and dancing, and the office parties— and the *food*—huh? Oh, my! Every stop on the way! It's safe to say that I'm glad most of the pants in my wardrobe have an elastic waistband at this time of year . . . hmm? Don't you feel the same way? Yes, yes, I know . . . day after New Year's and it is straight to the gym, and I'll see you there! Of course, the decorations that Lois and the Fat Man have strewn about this place are dreadful. But although they're aesthetically vacant, they do possess a certain degree of simple, understated charm. My favorite is a tacky, three-dimensional piece called an advent calendar. It's a small wooden façade of a rather large Victorian home, with many functioning shuttered windows. I guess the idea is to open a new window for every day that passes before Christmas, right up until the big day arrives. I've been having a ball with it, though, as I've taken time to draw bawdy little scenes to place in each window, and I've used the entire calendar to act out a self-composed tiny, but hilarious, British door-slamming farce. I keep trying to show it to Brian, but he can't bring himself to sit still long enough. It's not that he's excited about Christmas, it's just that yesterday the Fat Man dragged some sort of large pine shrubbery into the living room and Brian has spent every hour since then staring at it and resisting his canine urge to urinate on it, thereby marking it for his own. But I don't need that distracted imbecile's participation to enjoy my holi-day revelry. In fact, nothing has stopped me from having myself a holly-jolly time

What's so bad about getting coal in your stocking? With today's gas prices, I'm happy to start exploring reliable, alternative fuel sources. Bring it on, Klaus! Coal me up!

thus far. But lest you think that the spirit of goodwill toward all men has caused me to go soft, I will remind you that it was almost one year ago that my worthy adversary, and occasional ally, Mr. Klaus both procured and provided me with a small cache of weapons-grade plutonium. This I was able to garner from him on the agreement that during the Christmas season I would be a "good boy." Well, the corpulent gent made good on his word, so this year, I am once again taking the same course in the hopes of obtaining a functioning intercontinental missile-based delivery system. And if it works, good people, then let this be fair warning to you that it will be but a short matter of time before you will all BOW TO ME! So enjoy your holidays, for what may very well be your last time. Peace be with you! Fools.

## Christmas Thoughts from Brian

The holiday season has always presented me with mixed emotions. On the positive side it does provide a welcome break at the end of the calendar year, during which I can reflect on my life and make some honest choices about what I would hope to achieve for myself as I continue to grow and learn. On the negative side, Lois always makes me wear this very gay holiday sweater that she made for me. And in spite of the fact that I adore Lois, and by all accounts should be thrilled that such a woman of substance would take the time to knit me a sweater, the truth is that the thing is an eyesore, it's too small for me, and when I wear it, I look like a fat metrosexual Chihuahua who you'd expect to see peering out from Paris Hilton's handbag as she chats with the doorman outside the Skybar. And since you're asking me about it, I also bristle at the piety most people display at this time of year. There's always so much talk about people losing site of the fact that this holiday celebrates the birth of

Jesus. The truth is that what is now called Christmas was in fact a pagan holiday in ancient Rome that was centered around the winter solstice and was called the festival of Saturnalia. Its purpose was to pay homage to the sun, to express thanks for its warmth, and to encourage it to return with a plentiful spring. The ancient Romans danced with wreaths made of pine, which stayed green throughout the cold winter, and they decorated trees with apples and nuts as a sign of hope for the new season of growing that the sun would bring. Since it was too expensive to feed livestock through the winter, most animals were slaughtered, and the abundance of fresh meat resulted in a feast that was bigger than any they would have at any other time of the year. It wasn't until the fourth century that the church figured out they could get more people into the tent if they slapped their name on it, so they told everyone that Saturnalia was really about the birth of Jesus. And it worked, even though according to the Bible, Jesus was probably born in the fall, based on the simple fact that shepherds did not watch over their flocks in the winter, and also on some more intricate facts based on meteorological analogies, as well as the work of many noted astronomers. Peter often asks me why all of this bothers me so much and why I can't just shut my mouth and have a good time at Christmas. I tell him that it's just in my nature to rail against hypocrisy, and that it is in the best interest of all of us to question any authority, be it a church, or a government, a cult, or any entity that would subconsciously persuade us to surrender our own personal power. I tell him that, but it's really because I don't want to wear that stupid sweater. It's just so fucking embarrassing.

# Christmas Thoughts from Lois

**W**ell, hello there, everyone. Peter didn't tell me we were having company, but our home is always open at Christmastime. Or at any time, really, as far as Peter is concerned. One time he brought home a homeless man who was wearing a tinfoil hat and I actually ended up having to help Peter bathe him. I thought Peter was making a humanitarian gesture, but it turns out the bath was just a way for Peter to get the bum's pants off because he was curious to see what he had in his pockets. It was months before I could bring myself to get into that tub again. These are the things I go through. Our home is always a little crazy, but even more so at Christmas. There's so much to do. But I do love the holiday season. Or at least I did until last year, when I had a bit of an episode. I guess the stress of the holidays can really get to a person if you're not careful. I'm not saying there was any excuse for my behavior. I'm accountable for my actions. And I don't want to say anything negative about the dedicated members of the Quahog Police Department—some

of whom are among my closest friends. But I do question the practice of using tranquilizers that were manufactured primarily for cattle and livestock on a 105-pound housewife and mother of three—regardless of how high she climbed up on that Christmas tree in the center of Quahog, and regardless of who she punched out or kicked in the nuts on her rampage through town. And I would have forgiven all of that

so much quicker than it took me, if not for the fact that when I did hit the ground, unconscious, and was carried away to a waiting ambulance, the paramedics found some reason to take off my pants and underwear, something I learned weeks later only by seeing file footage of the event on the local news. Now, I can assure you that I'm fine with it all, and I can promise you that I've put it behind me, in spite of the fact that all during Christmas Peter looks at me as if I were a ticking bomb and that the whole time I've been talking to you he's been making wide-eyed "I'm scared" faces at you and doing a spinning "she's crazy" finger motion at his temple. I will not go crazy this year.

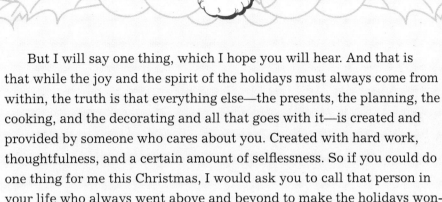
But I will say one thing, which I hope you will hear. And that is that while the joy and the spirit of the holidays must always come from within, the truth is that everything else—the presents, the planning, the cooking, and the decorating and all that goes with it—is created and provided by someone who cares about you. Created with hard work, thoughtfulness, and a certain amount of selflessness. So if you could do one thing for me this Christmas, I would ask you to call that person in your life who always went above and beyond to make the holidays wonderful and simply say, "Thank you." As much as giving is its own reward, I know that it would be a nice thing to hear. And I also know what it's like to spend four weeks on methadone to be eased off of bull tranquilizers, and I wouldn't want any other human being to go through it, especially during the holidays. Merry Christmas, from our home to yours.

## Christmas Thoughts from Peter

**W**hew! For a minute there, I thought she was gonna go all Margot Kidder on us. Okay, let's keep moving while we're playing with house money!

# Christmas Caroling: or "Wassailing," Whatever the Hell That Is

**A Christmas** tradition that's as old as Susan Sarandon is the festive ritual of caroling. It's name, "caroling" is a tribute to Carol Channing, the skinny, wide-eyed, gate-mouthed string puppet who's been the toast of Broadway since the American Revolution and who, once a year, took a rowdy theater crowd of drunks and ass-grabbers door to door through the streets of Manhattan, each singing songs of joy and happiness for the reward of a hot mug of cider and big hunks of cake. There are some of you out there—and yes, Perry Como, I mean you—who have also been caught on tape calling this custom "wassailing" or "a-wassailing," and it always confused the hell out of me. Last Christmas, Joe tried to tell me that "wassail" was some kind of Greek word for Christmas booze, or singing, or something, but Joe's one of those guys who always likes to pretend he's got the answer to stuff when he doesn't. It's a cop thing, I think, you know? Like he has to close every case, like a he's freakin' Kojak or something. But I have an easier explanation of why people would say "wassail" instead of "carol" and it's simply that when you're running around in the night, drinking and singing with your friends, it's just a matter of time before you start to get the words wrong. Like, "S'cuse me, while I

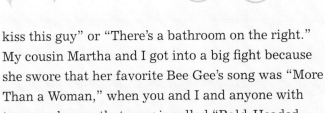

kiss this guy" or "There's a bathroom on the right." My cousin Martha and I got into a big fight because she swore that her favorite Bee Gee's song was "More Than a Woman," when you and I and anyone with two ears knows that song is called "Bald-Headed Woman." Stupid Martha. Bitch.

Anyway, I have gone caroling every year since I was a teenager and my high school hockey coach, Steve Nardelli, took us door to door as a team to sing to the citizens of Quahog. He showed up with a big accordion that his grandfather had given him and had taught him how to play. Coach said caroling would help us bond as a team, and it did, really. But even more helpful was the bottle of blackberry brandy that my friend Curt Lange brought along and that we were all taking turns swigging out of whenever Coach Nardelli wasn't looking because he was too busy playing the crap out of that accordion. And boy could he play! He was a real tough cookie on the ice, but man, you should have seen him out there on caroling night—smiling and singing and squeezing that thing in and out like Frankie Yankovic at a beer festival. It was such a surprise. But not as much as the one I gave him halfway through

Holiday fun fact: In certain circles Santa's "beard" was rumored to have been television legend Agnes Moorehead.

"Hark the Herald Angels Sing," because when I got to the "Glo-o-o-r-ia" part, the blackberry brandy kicked in and I threw up all over Coach and his grandfather's antique accordion. I think there was talk about my stomach acids doing permanent damage to the accordion's baffles, but whether or not that was true, I found myself cut from the hockey team the next morning. I didn't play too much hockey after that. But I have gone caroling every year since, and for that, I thank you, Coach Nardelli. To me there is nothing more fun than tooling around town with my best friends and drunkenly screaming songs into people's faces. Sure, sometimes there are arguments about which songs to sing. Cleveland, Quagmire, Joe, and I don't always agree. So, to help you start your own tradition this year,

I've asked my friends and family to each pick their favorite Christmas song to put on your "wassailing" list. Feel free to use any or all of these when you hit the streets with your pals. But remember—if anyone brings blackberry brandy, stop off at a Papa Gino's first and wolf down a couple of slices to sop up the booze in your gut. You're welcome! And happy wassailing!

# The Best Christmas Songs Ever

**Okay,** so here's what everybody said when I asked them to name their favorite Christmas songs. And just so you know, "White Christmas" isn't on here, because everybody already knows it's the best one ever, but also because on some level, it always makes Cleveland uncomfortable when we sing it at him.

**Lois** My choice would be "Have Yourself a Merry Little Christmas" by Judy Garland. The melody is so lovely, and the sentiment so charming, it's hard to believe this great performance was given by a woman horrifically addicted to booze and barbiturates.

**Chris** Mine is "Rockin' Around the Christmas Tree" by Brenda Lee. It speaks to a simpler time in America. Plus, when the part comes to sing "Deck the halls with boughs of holly," make sure you and your friends scream, "Check the balls on Uncle Charlie!" You'll thank me!

## Brian

I'd have to go with "Christmas Dream" by Perry Como. It's catchy and happy, and features Perry Como lazily singing along with a children's choir in a foreign language. The song was also heard in the opening scene of a 1970s film about Nazis called *The Odessa File*, which frankly gave the sound of happy German children's voices a rather disturbing tone.

## Meg

My favorite is "Christmas Wrapping" by the Waitresses. It's bouncy and fun, and has a great story about a lonely girl who can't get together with a guy she likes until "that Christmas magic" brings the tale "to a very happy ending." Shut up, Chris.

## Stewie

I would have to go with "I Believe in Father Christmas" by Greg Lake. Yes, the Greg Lake of Emerson, Lake & Palmer fame. Get the fully orchestrated version, as opposed to the acoustic track on ELP's *Works, Volume II* album. The arrangement is moving and builds to the foreboding lyric, "Hallelujah! Noel! be it Heaven or Hell / The Christmas we get, we deserve." Any guesses as to what *you'll* be getting this year?

## Cleveland

Hey y'all. For me, it just gets no better than "This Christmas" by Donny Hathaway. Smooth, funky, and a real hit with the ladies—much like Donny himself!

## Quagmire
If it's smooth you want, get "Baby, It's Cold Outside" by Bobby Caldwell and Vanessa Williams. Caldwell is a crooner who would've been a household name if it weren't for the fact that he looks like Bob Denver from *Gilligan*. And Vanessa had a nude spread in *Penthouse* that even had chicks going at her. Need I say more? Giggity!

## Joe
I'd be hard-pressed to find a better piece of music than "Fairytale of New York" by the Pogues. Also known as "Christmas in the Drunk Tank," this record artfully melds the beauty, nostalgia, and rage that to me have been the hallmark of every Christmas since my accident. There's also a nod to the boys in the NYPD choir, some of whom I am proud to call my friends.

## Mayor West
Hands down, my fave rave is "Christmas in Japan in July" by the Young Adults, a legendary Rhode Island combo that featured lead singer Rudy Cheeks, who frequently dressed in a Santa suit onstage and played the glockenspiel on this track. Good luck finding it, but if you can't, I will gladly come to your home and sing it to you repeatedly, while doing a wild, interpretive dance that I call "The Funky Pot Roast."

## The Greased-up Naked Deaf Guy
They all sound the same to me! See you all next year!

**Peter**   And I guess mine is a toss-up between Elmo and Patsy's "Grandma Got Run Over by a Reindeer" and the lesser-known "R2-D2 We Wish You a Merry Christmas." Brian found it at a yard sale, and the lead singer is rumored to be a young, pre-fame Jon Bon Jovi. Who cares? The song is awesome! If I were you I'd illegally download all of these as soon as possible. And when you're smiling and singing through your holiday season, you can thank your good friends from Quahog, and the faceless studio musicians and record industry workers who can't enjoy Christmas anymore because people like you are using your computers to steal from them.

# "The Night Before Christmas": in Quahog

**And** lastly, on Christmas Eve, when the rush is through, and the shopping is done, and all of the specials have aired, and there's nothing to watch on TV because most channels are showing the pope doing midnight mass at the Vatican or, even worse, *Ski Party*, with Frankie and Annette, I gather with my children and share a famous poem, that I always pretend to read from a book but I know it by heart. Which is good because not many people—let alone my children—know that I read at a third-grade level, so it wouldn't be long before frustration set in and I'd never get through it. It's a holiday classic that you also may know by heart. But, just in case, it goes like this:

There was a huge star in the East. A bigger Far East star than Jackie Chan or Lucy Liu. But not quite bigger than Kam Fong as "Chin Ho." For no star anywhere is bigger than Kam Fong as "Chin Ho." Except maybe Zulu as "Kono."

133

'TWAS the night before Christmas, and all through the town,

All the good folks of Quahog, were about to bed down.

Not a creature was stirring, not even a mouse,

Except for Glenn Quagmire, still up at his house.

He was stirring martinis, so nimble and quick,

And bragging about his big peppermint stick.

Cleveland, was snoozing, all loaded on beer,

When his snoring kicks in, you can hear him from here!

And Lois in her kerchief, and I in my cap,

And Brian on the front lawn, taking a crap.

The children were nestled, all snug in their beds,

While visions of Eve Plumb danced on their heads.

Then out through the window, I heard such a clatter,

And I saw a fat man—even though I was fatter.

His suit was so loud that it made him look queer,

And I knew that he sure didn't live around here.

I decided I'd go out and tackle this louse,

He was lucky I don't keep a gun in the house.

When, what to my wondering eyes should appear,

This fat-ass was hauling a whole keg of beer!

This guy wasn't some kind of burglar dick,

He wasn't a crook, he was big fat St. Nick!

A bundle of toys he had on his pack,

And his red suit had ridden right up his butt crack.

As he walked through the snow, he went down with a slip,

And his reindeer all laughed, so he took out his whip.

"Shut up, Mrs. Dash! Up yours, Tiny Dancer!

What the hell's so funny, huh? Give me the answer!"

The reindeer thought quick not to laugh anymore,

It was clear they had brushed with his temper before.

The sound of his yell nearly brought me to tears,

Like when we were canceled for four or five years.

But no one woke up, not one single kid,

Though he did wake up Lois, and that big giant squid.

So I said, "Listen, pal, you've had a long night,

If you just put the stuff down and go, that's all right."

He said, "Are the gifts really all that you care about?"

And I said, "Of course, you moron. It's Christmas, whaddaya think I've been waiting for all this time? What . . . ? What . . . you think I'm gonna sit down and hear all about your problems? You really think I want to get into all that? I got my own problems, you know? I don't want to hear yours. Go talk to your wife, because, I don't . . . I can't . . . And, and, even if I wanted to, *you* don't have the time. You gotta be at every other house in the world before dawn. So just gimme all our stuff and get the hell out of here." And I think he was refreshed by my honesty, so he did.

And I heard him exclaim as he drove out of sight,

"Merry Christmas to all, and to all a good night."

And I yelled back at him as he flew down the street,

"Merry Christmas, you bastard!" Freakin' sweet.

# Drinking

**So, how are you** feeling so far? Huh? Is that holiday spirit kicking in yet? I hope so, because it oughta be, with all the things we've seen and talked about already. I mean, okay, we still haven't figured out what the hell a damned Yule log is, but we have covered a lot of other stuff. We've heard great stories from the past, and happy thoughts from the present. And we've seen firsthand how the joyous customs of this great season are still practiced today, by decent, hard-working folks right here in my little northeast corner of the world. And besides all that—Santa's coming! Heh-heh-heh-heh-heh-heh-heh-heh-heh! Doesn't that get you a little stoked? I'm bettin' it does. Every time I even think about it, I can't stop myself from running in place and laughing hysterically and slapping my big red mittens together, over and over. That thought alone should fill your heart with so much warmth and excitement that somewhere down inside you, some frozen stuff starts to crack and melt, like the Winter Warlock's long bony fingers, or that huge glacier near Chile that's going to eventually flood all of Manhattan if it doesn't knock it off. But I understand that some people need more than others to get through this time of the year. And if you're still feeling lousy at this point, then there is only one thing left for you, and that is drinking.

Invented by Peter O'Toole, and brought to the New World by the

Germans, drinking is a holiday tradition as true and reliable as the lord himself. You may not find peace at Christmas, or patch up a long-standing dispute with a loved one, or patch the multiple holes in that stupid lousy inflatable snow globe that I want to kill Mort for charging me a freakin' hundred bucks for. But you can always get your hands on a case of beer, or something stronger, and numb all those nightmare hurts that chase you through the year and that are somehow always more powerful at Christmas.

No, it's not the answer. But it's a pretty damn good stall. And one that's pretty much accepted in our society, in spite of what a bunch of mother's groups and Betty Ford might have to say. You don't think so? Well, then riddle me this, Silas Marner—did you ever see an ad for crack cocaine during a football game? Nope. Ever see an ad for beer during a football game? Case closed. Like it or not, we live in a culture of drinking. And we should, because drinking is in the Bible. Look it up. They're always running around wasted, and waving palm trees around and making a joyful sound. And Jesus could make wine out of water, which means he and his buddies could get bombed any time they wanted, even if all the package stores were closed. But boy, it really is too bad there aren't ads for crack during football. Not because I'd ever want to do crack, but imagine those fancy Budweiser horses, all coked up and trying to have a touch football game in the snow? That'd be hilarious. Anyway, if all else fails at the holidays, I advise you to start drinking heavily. Drink responsibly, but heavily. It will take the edge off, it'll make all your big loud stories seem funnier, and it will definitely help you get through the next part of Mr. Magoo's journey—Christmas Yet to Come.

Part
Four

Christmas
Yet to Come

**Okay,** so it's the middle of the night on Christmas Eve, and poor old Mr. Magoo is really on the ropes, especially after the Ghost of Christmas Presents has shown him around the town, and now he knows that everybody pretty much thinks he's a dick. That would really suck, wouldn't it? I wouldn't wish that on anyone—even Angela, my boss down at the brewery. I mean, sure, I think she's a real aggot-smasher, and a very undesirable, angry hag, but I have always contended that my opinions of others are not necessarily any of their business, especially that man-hating hosebag. And by the way, Angela, if you're reading this, you look very lovely today. Anyway, just when Mr. Magoo figures he can't stands no more—as Popeye used to say—wouldn't he be damned if a *third* ghost doesn't show up in his freakin' room! And this third ghost is not messing around. In fact, he won't even talk to Mr. Magoo. I don't mean in that stuck-up way that twenty-something girls won't talk to you in the clubs, even though they're all dressed up in a way that really, *really* makes you want to talk to them, in spite of the fact that you're married and old enough to be their father. But they just stare right through you, like *you* were some kind of ghost, even when you just forked out almost thirty bucks to buy them a bunch of pink drinks like Sarah Jessica Parker is always swilling down on *Sex and the City*. And you realize that the only reason they're dressed

143

so wickedly hot is so you'll buy them free booze, and then they can all go out on the dance floor and dance with each other, then leave with some young unshaven Colin Farrell douche bag in a knit cap. Well, this Ghost isn't like that. This ghost is freakin' terrifying! And he's as mysterious as his name . . . the Ghost of Christmas Yet to Come.

Now, "Christmas Yet to Come" means that Mr. Magoo is about to be transported into his future. It's also the lighthearted name that Lois has for the brief sex we enjoy every Christmas Eve, right after we put out all the presents, which supports my long-standing and deep-seated belief that women are not funny. But I want to tell you right now that just as much as the Ghost of Christmas Past always shows you a good time, this part of the story always sucks. People are dead. Everybody's crying and miserable. Who the hell wants to see that? We don't need some scary, bony ghost to tell us that no matter what our story is, it's always gonna end with us taking a dirt nap. I mean, even Jesus—the guy who put the "Christ" in "Christmas"—look at how bad *his* story ended in the future, with him nailed to a telephone pole and a bunch of stupid Italian guys poking at him and laughing, and feeding him vinegar on a sponge. You think he wants to ruin his holiday by thinking about that? And even if we thought we weren't gonna die, we can't be sure that Christmas in the future will be anything to write home about. I mean, who knows—in the future, Santa Claus may be a reptiloid. Do you want that? Huh? Instead of a jolly old elf in a red suit, Santa Claus is a giant, two-legged lizardlike thing that spits acid? Like the dinosaur that killed Newman in *Jurassic Park*? Well, if you do, you're crazy. And sure, you wanna believe it's all gonna be better, with us all cruising around in our flying cars and eating cheeseburgers in pill form, which would be awesome, but I'm here to tell you that it won't be. And remember, even if it were, I am here specifically to help you enjoy *this* holiday season, not some made-up one down the road. You see, unlike your parents, or the government, I care about you, pal. And I don't want you to spoil your Christmas by looking too far into the future. It simply won't help. Because Christmas is like pooping. Think about it. When it's happening, there is nothing better. When it's over, it's kind of horrible, really. There's a big mess, and everything stinks, and depending on where it took place, some people might be mad.

And isn't that just like Christmas? Yes, it is! And it has always been this way. When we're babies, pooping and Christmas happen without our participation, and before we're even aware of it. The same can be said for when we're very old, or for that one time I was driving to New Haven with Lois and I made the poor choice of washing down a large steak dinner with a sixteen-ounce glass of orange juice. I guess that was more about pooping than Christmas, but it doesn't take away from the fact that Christmas, like pooping, is an experience we all share, whether we're ready or not. And no matter what we think, we have very little control over either one of them. For example, you could try to *not* poop when you really have to, but you're just gonna make yourself miserable, because poop knows better, and it's gonna happen. Or even worse, you can really *try* to poop when you're not able to, but that's dangerous, because it could possibly make you blow a gasket and croak on the toilet like Elvis did, or at the very least, launch a small cluster of painful hemorrhoids that'll hang from your button like a tiny bunch of grapes. So what are we to do? Well, Sparky, there's only one thing we can do, and that is to just relax and let it happen. Because Christmas and pooping don't happen to us—they happen *through* us. They're bigger than we can understand, and there is simply nothing like them. Especially pooping. It's the poor man's orgasm, really. And the only real way to enjoy them both is to stay in the moment. Let peace be with you. Savor the joy, the relief, and the warm satisfaction that are all such a part of both Christmas and pooping. Don't worry what happened in the past, or what might happen in the future. Don't grunt or strain, or shout and cry. Just stay in the eternal now, keep that great feeling with you in your heart, and I'm tellin' ya, you will always have a freakin' sweet time—at the holidays and all through the year. And the next time some lost and grouchy person comes up to you and says, "Christmas is crap!," well, you can nod wisely and say, "Yes, it is my friend. Yes, it is." And hey—maybe *that's* what a Yule log is all about! Wow. Merry Chrish-mish, everybody. Thank you, Mr. Magoo, wherever you are. And as the pale, sexually confused ukulele-playing falsetto crooner Tiny Tim once said on *The Tonight Show Starring Johnny Carson*, "Good night, Miss Vicki. And God Bless Us Everyone."

## Epilogue

# You've Got About a Week or So Before It All Gets Crappy Again

**Okay,** I think you're ready now, Cunningham. It's time for you to go running through the streets of your hometown and scream "Merry Christmas!" to everyone, like when Jimmy Stewart went off his nut in that movie. Or you could scream, "Live, live, live!" like Auntie Mame did to young Peggy Cass on the stairway of her wicked nice New York apartment, which I don't know how she could possibly have afforded unless she was a prostitute, which they did not show you in that movie. It's all up to you now. It's your holiday season. And while it's going on, I'd like you to remember something said to me by my old, Irish grandmother—whose wisdom was often hidden by the fact that she fell down a lot and frequently carried on conversations with the television. But when she wasn't doing those things, she always told me, "Peter . . . keep your head warm, and your feet warm—and never miss a minute."

So deck those halls! Ring those bells! Hit those malls! Smell those smells! Love and laugh so hard that you fall down into the snow and soil yourself. It's all about now, remember, and you *should* enjoy it now. Because it's only gonna be a matter of time until we're all back to work, and stuck in traffic, and hating our lives again. The Christmas tree will have morphed into a dried-out and highly flammable eyesore. The Christmas lights that we were so excited to take out of the garage and put up will soon be hopelessly tangled up in a large, snarly, brain-melting knot that we'll stuff into a box, leaving a huge headache for whoever has to deal with them next year. The same goes for the decorations, which eerily lose all their beauty and magic just a few days after New Year's. It's a lot like what happened to Kathleen Turner in the short years following *Body Heat*. But while she kept on making movies, those decorations are going straight into a big Tupperware tub in the garage. Except for the inflatable snow globe, which I'll leave in the yard, because I just remembered that I have a bicycle tire patch kit in the cellar somewhere, and I could pick a weekend sometime and really sit down and fix that thing. Meanwhile, there will be Christmas bills that no honest man can pay, and we'll slowly chip away at them all through the summer and into the fall, working so hard for money we've already spent a year ago. By then, your ass may once again be dragging, your spirits once again dimmed, and your soul again exhausted as you stare down the barrel of yet another Christmas. And when that happens, I assure you that just like E.T.—the Extra-Terrestrial, who bore a striking resemblance to the fleet-footed former St. Louis Cardinals outfielder Willie McGee, which any savvy sportscaster could have pointed out was only fitting, since Willie's play was, more often than not, truly "out of this world"—I will be right here. And together, we'll take that magic ride again. That is my promise, and my gift to you for every holiday season that we both have the privilege to share and enjoy. Just one thing, though . . . next time, do me a real big favor and keep your hands to yourself. Because whatever vibe I may be putting off, I'm really sorry, but I'm just not interested in you that way. See you next year!

# Acknowledgments

**W**riting this book has caused me to reflect back on three of the greatest gifts I've ever received at Christmas or any other time. In the late 1960s, my parents gave me a gift subscription to *Mad* magazine.

In the mid-1980s, my wonderful wife gifted me with a set of improv classes at the Groundlings Theater.

**A.**

And the third gift came in 1998, when I sat down for a job interview with a talented young animator named Seth MacFarlane. On that day, I felt immediately that I was in the presence of a kindred spirit. We made each other laugh, and I'm happy to say we've been working and laughing together ever since. *Family Guy* is a comedy writer's dream. Creatively, it's the most fun I've ever had, and it continues to be a gift that keeps giving, all thanks to that eccentric kid I met with the big thick glasses and the blue-and-red striped Rugby shirt nearly ten years ago. Much has been written about Seth's talent as an artist, writer, actor, and singer. In Hollywood, the word "genius" is often overused. But in the case of Seth MacFarlane, I really don't think it suffices. I can also tell you firsthand that he is fair, kind, appreciative, and a gentleman. But what has always impressed me most about Seth is his poise under tremendous pressure. The world of network television is a meat grinder of stress, ego, conflict, and

**B.**

anxiety. I have seen some real meltdowns through the years. But I have never seen anyone handle this business with such grace, patience, tact, and class as Seth MacFarlane. In that area, I have actually learned a lot from him, and I want to take this time to say, "Thanks a lot there, buddy." Thanks also for the laughs, for the tremendous creative outlet, and for making it possible for me to earn my livelihood by doing the very thing I used to get in trouble for doing back in high school, which is sitting around with a bunch of really funny bastards and laughing my ass off all day long.     —D.S.

C.

D.

**A.** *Young Seth MacFarlane exhibits genuine Christmas joy at the sight of a freshly unwrapped Transformer. Future hottie Rachel MacFarlane looks on.* **B.** *Young Danny Smith attempts humor by staging fake Christmas joy under a pile of Christmas treasures. Still looking for that Sandlot Slugger on e-Bay.* **C.** *Seth and Rachel MacFarlane on the lap of a Santa who they both suspect may very well be their father, Ron, based on his ratty Converse sneakers and the palpable aroma of weed.* **D.** *Danny Smith trims the tree on Orchard Avenue, years before his face and body would become ravaged by binge drinking and violent mood swings. Merry Christmas!*